Fortress • 61

Medieval Russian Fortresses AD 862–1480

Konstantin S Nossov • Illustrated by Peter Dennis

Series editors Marcus Cowper and Nikolai Bogdanovic

First published in 2007 by Osprey Publishing
Midland House, West Way, Botley, Oxford OX2 0PH, UK
443 Park Avenue South, New York, NY 10016, USA
E-mail: info@ospreypublishing.com

ISBN 978 1 84603 093 2

Editorial by Ilios Publishing, Oxford, UK (www.iliospublishing.com)
Cartography by The Map Studio, Romsey, UK
Design by Ken Vail Graphic Design, Cambridge, UK
Typeset in Monotype Gill Sans and ITC Stone Serif
Index by Alison Worthington
Originated by United Graphics, Singapore
Printed in China through Bookbuilders

07 08 09 10 11   10 9 8 7 6 5 4 3 2 1

A CIP catalogue record for this book is available from the British Library.

FOR A CATALOGUE OF ALL BOOKS PUBLISHED BY OSPREY MILITARY AND AVIATION PLEASE CONTACT:

Osprey Direct, c/o Random House Distribution Center, 400 Hahn Road, Westminster, MD 21157
Email: info@ospreydirect.com

Osprey Direct UK, P.O. Box 140, Wellingborough, Northants, NN8 2FA, UK
E-mail: info@ospreydirect.co.uk

www.ospreypublishing.com

Acknowledgements and image credits

The author wishes to express sincere thanks to Vladimir V. Golubev for creating the black and white illustrations that feature in this book. All the photographs in this book are from the author's collection. All permissions requests should be addressed to: konst-nosov@mtu-net.ru

Artist's note

Readers may care to note that the original paintings from which the colour plates in this book were prepared are available for private sale. All reproduction copyright whatsoever is retained by the Publishers. All enquiries should be addressed to:

Peter Dennis
Fieldhead
The Park
Mansfield
Nottinghamshire
NG18 2AT
UK
(email: magie.h@ntlworld.com)

The Publishers regret that they can enter into no correspondence upon this matter.

The Fortress Study Group (FSG)

The object of the FSG is to advance the education of the public in the study of all aspects of fortifications and their armaments, especially works constructed to mount or resist artillery. The FSG holds an annual conference in September over a long weekend with visits and evening lectures, an annual tour abroad lasting about eight days, and an annual Members' Day.
The FSG journal *FORT* is published annually, and its newsletter *Casemate* is published three times a year. Membership is international. For further details, please contact:

The Secretary, c/o 6 Lanark Place, London W9 1BS, UK
website: www.fsgfort.com

Contents

Introduction

According to the historical annals, in the year AD 862 Slav tribes called upon Varangian princes to come and rule over them. Three Varangian princes (whose names were Rurik, Sineus, and Truvor) arrived in Rus', bringing their troops along with them. Rurik settled in Novgorod, Sineus in Beloozero, and Truvor chose Izborsk (hence the name of the first fortified settlement in Izborsk – Truvor's *gorodishche*). The date indicated in the chronicle has, however, been recently called into question and the above developments are believed to have occurred somewhat earlier.

After the death of these princes, Prince Oleg, the guardian of Rurik's son Igor, seized Kiev and made it his capital, thus uniting the north Russian (Novgorodian) and south Russian (Kievan) lands. This event, which marked the birth of an early feudal state known as Kievan Rus', took place in 882. Prince Oleg and his successors carried out the policy of subjugation and the bringing together of various tribes; they launched several campaigns against Constantinople as well. This contact with the fortifications of Constantinople, which were among the strongest at the time, did not, however, have any visible impact on the evolution of Russian fortifications. As a result of the policy of expansion the territory of Kievan Rus' was considerably enlarged: in the 10th century it extended as far as the steppes off the banks of the Dnieper to the south of Kiev, and the Gulf of Finland and Lake Ladoga to the north.

The 11th century saw the beginning of feudal relationships in Rus', which were further consolidated towards the end of the century. Kievan Rus' as a political entity gradually disintegrated, breaking down into separate minor principalities. By the 13th century feudal disintegration had reached its apogee. The lack of unity between the princes made Rus' fair game for Mongol invaders, who

The Pskov *krom* (citadel) viewed across the River Pskova where the latter flows into the River Velikaya. The *krom* sits on the promontory at the confluence of the two rivers.

captured most of its territory including Kiev. Most Russian principalities found themselves as tributaries to the Golden Horde.

The territory of the feudal principalities of that time can be divided into four large regions: south Rus' (the lands in the area of the mid-section of the River Dnieper); west Rus' (the Galich and Volhynia principalities); north-west Rus' (the Novgorod and Pskov lands); and north-east Rus' (the principalities of Vladimir and Suzdal). The territories of south Rus' and north-east Rus' were devastated by the Mongols, and the building of fortifications would cease for several centuries to come. The principalities of west and north-west Rus' fared better, and it is here that we can perceive the main tendencies in the further evolution of fortifications in Rus'.

The Mongol armies used advanced siege weapons and standard siege methods learnt in the course of their wars in Central Asia and China. It was in this way that the Russians became acquainted with Eastern siege warfare. At the same time both the fortifications and siege weapons of the north-western part of Rus' evolved, in the midst of frequent armed conflicts with German, Swedish, and Lithuanian armies throughout the 13th and 14th centuries. It was here that the Russians became acquainted with European methods of siege warfare.

The beginning of the 14th century saw the rise and growth of the Moscow principality, at the expense of nearby principalities. In 1328 Prince Ivan Kalita of Moscow obtained dispensation from the Golden Horde attesting his right to rule as the 'Great Prince'. The Moscow principality now formed the political centre of all the Russian principalities – a status previously enjoyed by Vladimir. From that time on, the title of 'Great Prince' was held by Moscow princes only.

A wall and the Malaya Tower of Porkhov fortress. The wall is topped with broad, rectangular merlons but lacks loopholes. The space beneath the wall was commanded through the loopholes of the tower. The square apertures are put-log holes, which supported duckboards during the construction of the fortress.

The borders of Kievan Rus', and the locations of the fortified settlements mentioned in this book.

In the second half of the 14th century the reinforced Moscow principality was powerful enough to be able to offer armed resistance to the Golden Horde. However, it would take a hundred years for the country to be freed from the Mongol yoke. The process was only brought to conclusion in 1480 when Great Prince Ivan III (1462–1505) proclaimed himself Tzar and trampled down the Khan's charter. In the battle that followed in 1480, the two armies stood facing each other across the River Ugra for a long time, neither daring to attack the other, before the Mongol army finally retired. The result was the emergence of an independent Russian state, whose history has been dealt with in Fortress 39: *Russian Fortresses 1480–1682.*

Chronology

AD 862   Slav tribes call upon Varangian (Scandinavian) princes to come and rule over them. The event is mentioned in the annals of this year, however it may have happened a little earlier.

882–912   Prince Oleg rules in Kiev.

907   Russian armies led by Oleg march on Constantinople.

912–45   Prince Igor rules in Kiev.

915   Pechenegs make their first raid on Rus'.

941–44   Prince Igor conducts campaigns against the Byzantines.

957–72   Prince Svyatoslav rules Rus'.

968   The siege of Kiev by Pechenegs. Besieged on all sides, the inhabitants are close to starvation when Prince Svyatoslav and his army come to the rescue.

Interior view of a wall and a loophole of the *boevoy hod* (wall-walk) in the Pskov *krom*. Pskov's defensive walls lack merlons and crenellations. The parapet is solid and fire was only effected through loopholes.

980–1015	Prince Vladimir rules in Kiev.
988	The adoption of Christianity (baptising of Rus').
989	A new fortified enclosure known as 'Vladimir's city' is under construction in Kiev.
1019–54	Prince Yaroslav the Wise rules in Kiev.
1037	Prince Yaroslav completes the construction of the new fortified enclosure in Kiev called 'Yaroslav's city', following 15–20 years' work.
1055	The Polovtsy make their first appearance on the south-east borders of Rus'.
1068	The regiments of the Russian princes are defeated by the Polovtsy on the River Alta, near Pereyaslavl.
1096	The Polovtsy raid Kiev.
1113–25	Prince Vladimir Monomakh rules in Kiev. The prince conducts several successive campaigns against the Polovtsy, stopping their raids on Rus' for some time.
1169	Prince Andrei Bogolyubski devastates Kiev.
1176–1213	Prince Vsevolod of the Big Nest rules in the Vladimir-Suzdal principality.
1223	The combined Russian–Polovetsian troops suffer a crushing defeat at the hands of the Mongols in the battle of the Kalka River.
1237–38	The hordes of Batu Khan seize and lay waste to Ryazan, Moscow, Vladimir, Kozelsk, and other Russian towns and cities.
1238	Russian armies are defeated in the battle on the River Sit'.
1239–40	The Mongols invade southern Rus'; they capture Pereyaslavl, Chernigov, Kiev, and other cities.
1240	The Novgorodian prince Alexander routs the invading Swedish army on the River Neva, which wins him the nickname of 'Nevski'. The Teutonic Knights (German crusaders) seize Izborsk by assault and then Pskov through treachery.
1242	Alexander Nevski defeats the Teutonic Knights in the battle of Lake Peipus.
1262	Risings against the Mongols in Rostov, Vladimir, Suzdal, Yaroslavl, and Ustyug are brutally put down.
1265–1300	Prince Dovmont rules in Pskov. A new defensive wall is built here during his rule, forming 'Dovmont's city'.
1301	The Moscow principality absorbs the city of Kolomna.
1302	The Pereyaslavl principality is annexed by the Moscow principality.
1303	The Moscow principality absorbs Mozhaisk.
1325–40	Prince Ivan Kalita rules in Moscow.
1328	Prince Ivan Kalita of Moscow obtains dispensation from the Golden Horde attesting his right to rule as Great Prince, thus making the Moscow principality the political centre of all the Russian principalities.
1339–40	The Moscow Kremlin acquires new oak fortifications.
1348	Pskov officially becomes independent from Novgorod.
1367	A white-stone *kremlin* is built in Moscow.
1378	Russian armies defeat the Mongols on the River Voje.
1380	Russian armies defeat the Mongols at Kulikovo Field.
1382	Khan Tokhtamysh of the Golden Horde reaches Moscow and burns it to the ground. The Russians use cannon in defence – the first use of firearms by Russians mentioned in the annals.
1408	The invasion of Khan Edigu of the Golden Horde. The Mongols besiege Moscow.
1462–1505	The rule of Prince Ivan III. A new, brick, Italian-style *kremlin* is built in Moscow (1485–95), the first of the 'Italian style' to appear in Russia.
1471	The Novgorodians are defeated by the troops of Ivan III on the River Shelon.
1478	The Moscow principality annexes Novgorod.
1480	Ivan III refuses to pay tribute to the Golden Horde, resulting in a confrontation on the River Ugra, the casting off of the Mongol yoke, and the emergence of an independent Russian state.

The principles of defence

The types of fortified settlement

In medieval Rus' a fortified settlement was called a *gorod* (or *grad*), as distinct from an unfortified one, which was usually called a *ves'* or *selo*. The word *gorod* was also used in a broader sense – meaning 'defensive walls', and fortifications in general.

Some 400 *gorods* are described in the historical annals and other sources; many more have been discovered by archaeological work. A virtually complete list of fortified settlements, compiled by A. V. Kuza, details 1,306 fortified settlements dating from the 10th to the mid 13th century; this number will be henceforth used when calculating the percentages of different types of *gorod*. With the inclusion of earlier settlements, those ravaged by the passing of time, and those still to be investigated by archaeologists, the number of fortified settlements in Rus' may well have been as high as 1,500 by the mid 13th century. Unfortified settlements greatly outnumbered fortified ones.

The fortified settlements may be divided into several types according to their social status:

- **Towns and cities**, i.e. centres of craft, trade and culture. The modern Russian word for town or city is *gorod* but its meaning is not identical to that of the Old Russian word: it now means only a town proper, not a country settlement nor a fortification. Old Russian towns had a specific structure: they comprised a citadel, which was originally called a *detinets*, and an adjoining trading settlement, called an *okol'ny gorod* or *possad*. Each was enclosed within defensive walls, so a town consisted of at least two fortified sites. The *detinets* was always the oldest part of the town. It was also the most important part, being the last place of refuge in its defence. Accordingly, its fortifications were much more powerful than those of the *okol'ny gorod*.
- **Fortified villages** were communal settlements. The fortifications were simpler in layout and more subject to the terrain.
- A **castle** was a fortified residence of a prince or boyar (aristocrat). A product of the feudal system, castles became widespread with the growth of feudal disunity in the 11th century, and disappeared in the 15th and 16th centuries with the formation of a centralized Russian state. A sharp increase in the number of fortified settlements in the 11th–early 12th centuries (a four-fold increase) and then again between the mid 12th and the mid 13th centuries (a 2.5-fold increase) can be attributed to the appearance of a large number of feudal castles. Many castle sites gradually grew into towns or cities, with the castle itself becoming the *detinets* – as happened at Moscow. There was no specific term for a castle in the Russian annals of the 10th–14th centuries.

The *gorodishche* of Kleshchin sits on a hill called Alexander's Mount. By the side of this small fortress was an unfortified settlement.

The rampart of Pereyaslavl (Pereyaslavl-Zalesski). Until the 13th–14th centuries Russian fortress-towns looked imposing. An outsider could see nothing but high earthen ramparts topped with wooden walls. People still live inside this rampart but their small houses are invisible from the outside.

A castle was called either a *gorod* (*grad*) or *dvor*. While the former word was a common name for all fortified settlements, the latter was used to describe country castles and town estates. The modern Russian word for castle – *zamok* – appeared later and is a derivative of the Polish word *zamek*. It is interesting to note that today in many Slavic languages this word does not mean castle. For example, the Czech word *zámek* means 'palace' (or unfortified residence), while a castle (fortified residence) is called a *hrad* (a word linked to the Old Russian *grad* or *gorod*).

- **Frontier fortresses** were fortified settlements with a military garrison in situ. These fortresses were usually built on the frontiers of a principality, on the borderline with the steppe, and other suitable places. The remains (*gorodishche*) of such fortresses are generally minimal as a rule, and do not indicate that one site was wealthier than the others (unlike castles). No special word for this kind of fortress existed in medieval Rus'. Like other fortified settlements, they were simply called *gorod*. It was not until the 17th century that the modern Russian word *krepost'* came into being. The term 'fortress' will henceforth be used in this book in a broader sense, as a synonym for a stronghold, unless specified that it refers to a frontier fortress with a military garrison.

- **Refuge fortresses**, characteristic of the north-west districts of Rus'. Unpopulated in times of peace, these fortresses were filled with the inhabitants of the neighbouring villages in times of danger. The emergence of these refuge fortresses is explained by the small sizes of villages in those districts. Some villages comprised only a few homesteads, and it was beyond their ability and means to protect themselves with even the most primitive fortifications. Therefore, several villages united to build a fortress. Refuge fortresses are known to have existed in the 10th and 11th centuries, but became rare after this, as with the appearance of numerous towns, castles, and frontier fortresses they were no longer in demand.

- **Monasteries**, which were built widely from the second half of the 14th century onwards. As soon as it was founded, a monastery was usually encircled by defensive walls; their fortifications were mostly wooden up to the 16th–17th centuries.

Nearly half of all the fortified settlements dating from the 10th to the 13th centuries were very small, with the fortified territory not exceeding 0.3 hectares. Most of these small settlements are considered to be feudal castles. Sometimes, however, castles occupied a much larger site (up to 1 hectare or larger), approaching towns in size. These larger castles (i.e. those occupying from 0.3 to 1 hectares) were particularly popular in southern Rus', mainly in the area around the mid-point of the River Dnieper. Fortified settlements of more than 2.5 hectares are generally referred to as towns.

The layout of fortified settlements

An analysis of surviving *gorodishches* allows us to single out several types of layouts for fortified settlements:

- **Insular layout**. The settlement was situated on an island in the middle of a river or marsh, or on a hill protected by ravines on all sides. Earlier settlements of this type generally had no earthen fortifications. In most cases nothing was done except for scarping the slopes of the hill. Later settlements (from the 11th century on) found themselves protected with a rampart all along the perimeter.

Truvor's *gorodishche* viewed from the rampart. The *gorodishche* sits on a pointed promontory formed by deep, steeply sloping ravines.

Settlements of this type had several shortcomings: the size of a settlement was limited by the size of the island; and communication between its inhabitants and the surrounding area was inhibited by its insularity. This type of settlement was unsuitable for people engaged in agriculture or livestock-breeding, and was thus more characteristic of refuge and frontier fortresses.

- **Cape layout**, or **simple cape layout**. The settlement occupied a promontory formed by the confluence of two rivers, or the junction of a river and a ravine, or two ravines coming together. Protected on two sides with water or steep slopes of the ravines, the settlement was open on the third, mainland side. It was this, the most vulnerable side, that received the principal fortifications – a ditch and a rampart surmounted with a wall. If a promontory featured a gentle slope to its tip, the latter was sometimes separated from the rest of the settlement with a ditch and a rampart. There could be up to three or four lines of defence (i.e. ditches and ramparts) on the mainland side as well as on the side of the tip of the promontory. Later, an entire settlement was surrounded with a rampart that was usually higher and steeper on the mainland side. Such settlements with a rampart running all along the perimeter first appeared at the end of the 10th century but became particularly popular in the 11th–13th centuries. The cape layout had considerable advantages compared to the insular layout. It offered better communications between the settlement and the neighbouring lands, and the possibility of extending the site of a settlement as the population grew; a suitable promontory was also much easier to find than a suitable island. Moreover, its defences could be raised with only a moderate employment of labour as two sides were already well protected with natural obstacles. All this made the cape layout the most popular type of settlement.
- **Segment layout**. The settlement sat on an isthmus, usually bordered by water on two sides. It was protected with ramparts and ditches on the two opposite mainland sides. This type was comparatively rare.
- **Complex cape layout**. The settlement was situated on a promontory and conformed to the terrain, but unlike the simple cape layout it comprised

Truvor's *gorodishche* and an earthen rampart. The settlement was fortified with a defensive wall along the entire perimeter; however, only the most vulnerable, mainland side featured a rampart and a ditch.

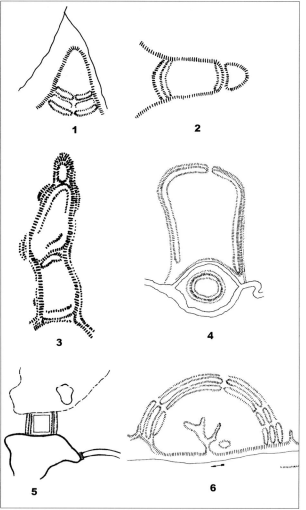

Several plans of *gorodishches* (not to scale): 1 – the simple cape type with two ramparts on the mainland side (near Rubtsovo village); 2 – the simple cape type with ramparts on the mainland side and at the tip of the cape (Strelitsa); 3 – the complex cape type with a circular rampart on the first site and ramparts and ditches edging two sides on the second site (Kvetun); 4 – the complex type with a citadel on a hill and a *possad* protected with a rampart (Korshov); 5 – the segment type (Yagotin); 6 – the semi-circular type with three lines of ramparts and ditches (Borisov-Glebov, or Romanovo-Borisoglebskoe *gorodishche*).

more than one site, each protected with its own defensive lines. The most heavily fortified part of the settlement, the *detinets* (citadel), was at the very tip of the promontory. The enemy had to seize the outer fortifications first, and only then could tackle the *detinets*. This type of fortified settlement appeared in the 10th century.

- **Complex layout**. The settlement comprised several fortified sites, as per the complex cape layout, but the defences of the outermost sites were independent of the terrain. The *detinets* was usually on the promontory, or, more rarely, on a small island. The rampart of the *okol'ny gorod* or *possad* (the external site) was never close to the ramparts of the *detinets*. Moreover, the outer site was never protected with a rampart on the side of the citadel. *Gorodishches* featuring complex layouts are generally considered to be the remains of large cities where a cape layout could not be strictly adhered to owing to quickly expanding trading areas (the *okol'ny gorod*). Hence the fortifications of the *okol'ny gorod* seldom conformed to the terrain and had no definitive layout; their task was only to protect the vast trading area. This layout may be regarded as the next stage in the development of a town, as compared to the complex cape layout. Settlements of a complex layout began to gain popularity in roughly the late 10th and early 11th centuries.

- **Circular layout**. Circular and oval settlements, widespread in the 12th century, were known earlier (beginning in the 10th and 11th centuries) in some districts. As a rule, they were situated in a valley and did not depend on the terrain. They were mostly small in size, with a diameter varying from 50 to 100m. One or more formidable earthen ramparts and ditches ran all along their perimeter.

- **Semi-circular layout**. This type of settlement bordered a river or a steep slope on one side and was protected with semi-circular ramparts and ditches on the other sides. Thus, it was only partially dependent on the terrain.

With certain assumptions, a connection can be made between a particular layout and the social status of a settlement. For instance, both a complex cape layout and a complex layout were on the whole typical of the defences of large cities. The complex cape layout can also be considered as a certain stage in the development of a city – from a simple cape layout through a complex cape layout to a complex layout. The simple cape layout and the insular layout were typical of fortified communal settlements, castles, and small towns. A cape layout is also characteristic of frontier fortresses. Settlements of semi-circular and circular layout were usually the castles of princes and boyars. There were of course numerous exceptions to these general rules.

The most common type of fortified settlement was one having a simple cape layout. Half of all the listed fortified settlements (654 out of 1,306) belong to this type. It was only in some western Russian districts that an insular layout was as common, or more prevalent. However a larger number of settlements of insular layout were not surrounded by water but sat on free-standing hills with steep slopes. The number of fortified settlements on islands proper, i.e. land surrounded by a river or a marsh, is insignificant (a mere 15 out of 1,306). Fortified settlements where natural obstacles played little or no part (i.e. those

of circular or semi-circular layout) account for 13.5 per cent of the total number of examined *gorodishches*. Fortified settlements of a complex cape or complex layout constitute 20.2 per cent of all fortified settlements. A third of all fortified settlements featured an unfortified one next to them.

General trends and territorial differences

Fortified settlements in the territory of medieval Rus' are known to have existed from the Bronze Age (the second millennium BC). The second half of the first millennium BC saw a significant increase in the number of fortified settlements as compared with unfortified ones. Examination of old, pre-Slavic settlements is beyond the limits of this work. It should, however, be noted that, like early fortified Slavic settlements, they sat on hilltops or high up the banks on a bend in a river (insular or simple cape layout), and that their defences consisted of ditches and ramparts surmounted with primitive wooden walls (mostly palisades). Many of these pre-Slavic fortified settlements were later used by Slavs, who usually modernized the fortifications by increasing the height of the ramparts and building new wooden walls on top of them.

The earliest authentic Slavic settlements date back to the 6th century AD. Most of the Slavic settlements of the 6th and 7th centuries were not fortified; however, the situation rapidly changed in the 8th century. A large number of settlements were realized, protected not only by the terrain but by artificial defences as well (ditches, ramparts, and palisades). Several unfortified settlements can often be

NEXT PAGES **Russian fortresses**
1 – Vladimir in the 12th–13th centuries; 2 – Suzdal in the 13th century; 3 – Ladoga in 1114; 4 – Kamenets in the late 13th century; 5 – Mstislavl in the early 13th century; 6 – the citadel of Tustan fortress in the 14th century; 7 – Porkhov fortress in the second half of the 15th century. One of the greatest Russian cities, Vladimir (**1**) became capital of the Vladimir-Suzdal principality in the mid 12th century. In the 12th and 13th centuries the city had four sites protected with walls; with a stone *detinets* (citadel) in its southern part, 'Monomakh's city' occupied the centre and was flanked by two fortified *possads*. Apart from the *detinets*, some of the gates were of stone too, including the famous Golden Gate. Suzdal (**2**) was another powerful city in north-east Rus' and capital of the Rostov-Suzdal principality in the first half of the 12th century. By the 13th century the city comprised a *detinets* enclosed by a wooden log wall and an *okol'ny gorod* protected by a *tyn*. Ladoga fortress (**3**, after E. G. Arapova and A. N. Kirpichnikov) saw its fortifications built in stone as early as 1114, thus becoming the first stone fortress in northern Rus'. Kamenets (**4**, after E. Kulik) is a typical fortress with a donjon-tower. Fortresses with independently standing towers became popular in the Galich-Volhynia principality in the second half of the 13th century. Mstislavl (**5**, after P. A. Rappoport) is a castle of an almost regular round shape. It stands in a valley and its fortifications do not conform to the terrain at all. Tustan (**6**, after M. F. Rozhko) is the best-known rock fortress in Galicia. The five-storey living quarters and the defensive walls with towers nestle between four rock projections. Porkhov (**7**, after E. G. Arapova and A. N. Kirpichnikov) was a frontier fortress of Novgorod. Founded in 1387, the fortress was more than once modernized up to the second half of the 15th century.

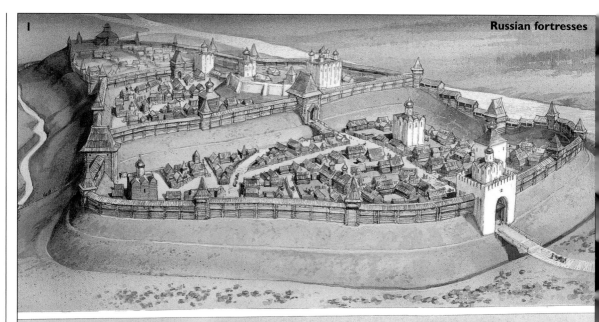

The rampart of Mstislavl. An oak intra-rampart structure has been discovered inside it. Wooden walls stood on top of the rampart, which was steeper on the exterior than on the interior. Grass, bushes, and trees on the outer side and in front of the rampart were destroyed in times of danger to prevent the enemy from hiding in them or more easily climbing the rampart.

found on the outskirts of these fortresses, which signifies that the fortresses served as residences of tribal chiefs and gave shelter to the neighbouring population in times of need.

The major threat to the southern Russian lands from the 10th through to the 12th centuries came from nomadic warriors. From the first half of the 10th century to the first half of the 11th century these were the Pechenegs, followed by the Torks; the mid 11th century brought the Polovtsy. The Pechenegs had crossed the River Volga and invaded the lands to the north of the Black Sea late in the 9th century. They settled within a day's march of the southern borders of Rus', making regular raids on her territory to seize booty and prisoners. The first clash between the Russians and the Pechenegs took place in 915. For more than a century (up to the year 1036) the Pechenegs continually attacked Rus'; in 968 they even besieged and nearly captured Kiev, the capital of Old Rus'. The Polovtsy proved to be no less deadlier an enemy, and first appeared on the south-east Russian borders in 1055. At the end of the 1060s a large-scale invasion was staged by the Polovtsy on Russian lands, and in the last decade of the century not a single year passed without a raid taking place.

The bulk of the nomad armies consisted of irregular cavalry. They did not know how to properly besiege a fortified place, and rarely engaged in sieges; when they did conduct them, they were seldom successful. As a result, the rulers of Kievan Rus' fortified existing cities and built frontier fortresses. The nomadic warriors rarely conducted raids inside enemy territory, fearing that the garrisons of any Russian fortress to their rear would attack them from behind or cut off their retreat. Lines of fortresses were built along the main frontier rivers – the Sula, the Stugna, the Ros', the Trubezh, the Desna and others. Another line of fortresses stretched along both sides of the River Dnieper, from the River Ros' as far as Kiev. These fortresses formed a second line of defence and were able to warn the capital city of Kiev of a breakthrough by the enemy hordes well in advance. Fortresses were also built along the routes of potential enemy movement – highways, river fords, and so on. In addition to these fortresses, extensive fortification lines – the Zmievy Valy – were created.

In the late 11th–early 12th centuries Rus' experienced a period of feudal disruption. A weakening of the authority of the Kievan princes and the disintegration of a once united state into independent principalities necessitated changes in Russian defensive strategy. With the incessant strife forcing each principality to defend its own frontiers, Russian princes began to make use of nomadic tribesmen to protect their land from the raids of other nomads. Back in the mid 11th century Pechenegs, Torks, and Berendeis had been allowed to settle in the border areas. These settlers, known as Chernye Klobuki (Black Hoods), served as a sort of barrier between the steppe and Rus'. In exchange for land they were obliged to participate in military operations against the enemies of Rus'. From that point onwards, raids by the Polovtsy were repulsed by united actions of Chernye Klobuki and Russians, or by Chernye Klobuki alone under the command of a Russian *voivode* (commander). In addition to defensive warfare, retaliatory raids into the steppe to drive out the Polovtsy from their camps took place from the turn of the 11th–12th century. Vladimir Monomakh and his son Mstislav were especially successful in the elaboration of these tactics.

The second half of the 12th century saw the construction of numerous fortifications comprising two to four parallel rows of ramparts and ditches. Some date from as early as the 10th and 11th centuries, when they were built with the aim of forcing the enemy to overcome one defensive line after another. However, in the 13th century they became especially important owing to the ever-increasing use of (initially stone) throwing machines, which could cause serious damage to wooden fortifications. Man-powered stone-throwing machines possessed real destructive power at a distance of 100–150m. Counterweight stone-throwers were more powerful, but were only effective at a distance of up to 200m. The chief target of a stone-thrower was the main defensive wall. In multi-row fortifications of the 13th–14th centuries ramparts were usually raised some distance away from each other. Together with ditches they created a defensive belt of considerable depth; for example, in Galich the defensive belt of four lines of ramparts and ditches was 92m deep. Therefore, in order to force the enemy to repeatedly use stone-throwers against the main (most formidable) wall they would have to be placed as near as 50–100m from the external defensive line. However, the soldiers manning these machines would thus be exposed to multi-tiered fire from the defenders, particularly from the outermost defensive line. All this forced the besiegers to tackle several defensive lines one after the other.

A typical defensive layout with three rows of fortifications consisted of the following elements. The first rampart had a very wide *boevoy hod* or wall-walk (20–32m) intended for archers mounted on horseback. The *boevoy hod* of the second rampart was narrower, at 2–9m. Both ramparts were usually topped with simple fortifications, such as a palisade or fence, or less commonly wooden log walls. The third defensive line comprised the main fortress wall. This line (which consisted of a rampart and a log wall as a rule) was two or three times higher than the first two. Each rampart was fronted with a ditch, with the inner ditches wider than outer ones. While the ditch in front of the outward rampart was generally 7–8m wide, the one fronting the middle rampart was between 6 and 14m wide, with the ditch in front of the inner rampart some 14–15m wide. Multi-row fortifications were not usually raised around the whole of a settlement, only on its most vulnerable mainland side. The mounting of throwing machines on the remaining sides was hindered by natural barriers, such as rivers, ravines, marshes, and the like. A single defensive line was thus often deemed sufficient.

Even when faced with the threat of a Mongol invasion, the Russian princes were unable to unite, and Rus' fell easily to the Mongol hordes, who subjugated most of its territory between 1237 and 1240. Many towns and cities were completely destroyed, never to be repopulated again, while others were ordered to pull down their fortifications with a watchful eye kept on them lest they be restored. Fortification building ceased for centuries in many districts, except for in the west (Galich-Volhynia principality) and north-west (Novgorod and Pskov areas), which escaped the Mongol yoke.

The Galich-Volhynia principality, formed in 1199 from the amalgamation of the Galich and Vladimir-Volhynia principalities, contained numerous remarkable fortresses, including two unique types not found elsewhere in Russian lands: fortresses with donjon-towers (mainly characteristic of Volhynia), and rock fortresses and castles (in the Carpathian mountains of Galicia). The

The fields of fire in a fortress of the 10th–12th centuries (A), and of the 14th to the first half of the 15th century (B). Earlier fortresses, having no towers, were only adapted to frontal fire. The 14th century saw the appearance of a new type of fortress with towers on the mainland side and straight curtain walls (*pryaslos*) in between. Thus, both frontal and flanking fire could be laid down on the mainland side, but only frontal fire on the other side.

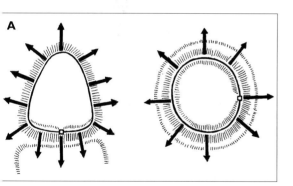

A

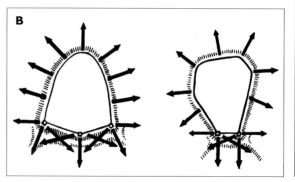

B

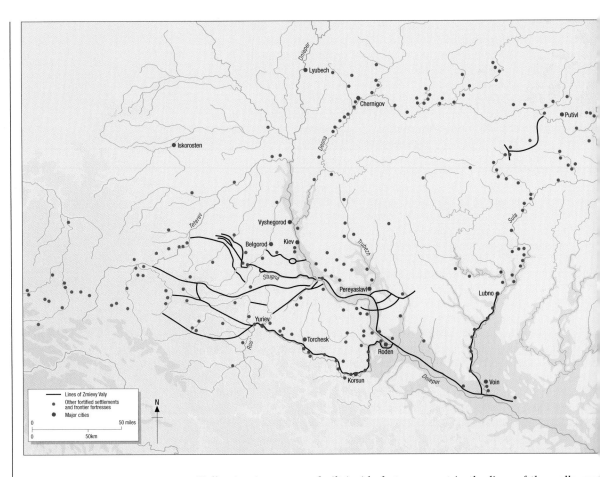

The Zmievy Valy (Snake Ramparts), 10th–11th centuries.

Volhynian towers were built inside fortresses, not in the lines of the walls, and had the same functions as donjons in western Europe. They were frequently built of stone or brick – even when all the other fortifications were wooden. Donjon towers became widespread in Volhynia in the second half of the 13th century, the result of the influence of its western neighbours Poland and Hungary. Examples of these towers survive in Berestie, Kamenets, Stolpie and Czartoryisk. Out of all the rock fortresses in the Carpathian mountains, Tustan fortress has undergone the most careful examination. Its central point, called *Kamen* ('Stone'), sat on rocks towering 51m above the surrounding valley. Wooden walls with towers and a five-storey (including the ground floor) building housing living quarters were all built on the rocks.

The north-west Russian district (comprising the Pskov and Novgorod lands) frequently found itself at war with the Teutons, Swedes and Lithuanians in the 13th and 14th centuries. This affected both the fortifications and defensive strategy. To protect their lands Novgorod and Pskov (which became independent from Novgorod in 1348) built a number of fortresses in the most vulnerable northern, western and southern areas. Among them were the fortresses of Izborsk, Porkhov, Kopor'e, and Oreshek. Stone (as opposed to

OPPOSITE **The construction of a Zmiev Val (Snake Rampart)**

In order to protect Kievan Rus' against raids by nomadic warriors, Prince Vladimir (r. 980–1015) built defensive lines of enormous extent (800–1,000km). These defence lines consisted of a ditch and an earthen rampart topped with a wooden wall. Numerous parts of the ramparts had a wooden intra-rampart structure to make them higher and steeper. The ditch ran along the rampart on its outer, steppe-facing side or, occasionally, on both sides. The Zmievy Valy began to be raised in the late 10th century and construction continued through the 11th century.

The construction of a Zmiev Val (Snake Rampart)

wooden) fortifications became increasingly common in these lands in the 14th century. At the beginning of this century the cities of Novgorod and Pskov were protected by masonry defences. The eastern areas, where the frontiers between the Novgorod lands and other Russian principalities lay, witnessed little fortress building. Fortresses were also extremely rare on the frontier between Pskov and Novgorod, despite rather cool relations and even the occasional military conflict between them.

North-eastern Rus' suffered greatly during the Mongol invasion; no new fortresses were built there from the mid 13th through to the mid 14th century; only pre-existing ones were restored. The 14th century was marked by the rise in power of the Moscow principality, which successfully expanded its territory by annexing neighbouring lands. With the frontiers of the principality constantly changing, it was not considered worthwhile to provide them with defensive military works, and the Moscow princes set about building and strengthening fortresses on the main routes leading to Moscow. Particular importance was now attached to Mozhaisk in the west, Kolomna in the south-east, Dmitrov in the north-west, and Serpukhov in the south. Moreover, practically all the cities around Moscow were fortified. Most villages, too, were defended with ditches, ramparts and wooden walls as a rule. Within a 50km radius of Moscow alone there were up to 40 *gorods* with ditches and ramparts. Of great importance was the strengthening of the capital itself. Between 1339 and 1340 the Moscow Kremlin saw its fortifications rebuilt of oak, and in 1367 it was given stone walls.

It is interesting to note that, unlike in the cities of north-western Rus', in the cities of the north-eastern Russian principalities only the fortifications of the *detinets* (citadel) were redeveloped, but not those of the *okol'ny gorod* (suburb). Moreover, there were no new outer defensive walls raised in north-east Russian cities during the 14th and 15th centuries, and even the old defences of the 12th and 13th centuries were not rebuilt. This lack of attention towards the cities' outer fortifications was probably a consequence of failures in the respective municipal governments, who were responsible for maintaining these defences; princes were more concerned with the construction and modernization of *detinets*. In Novgorod and Pskov municipal government was a powerful force; thus, these cities saw their old urban fortifications regularly rebuilt and new ones erected.

Multi-row fortifications were not often built in the Moscow and other principalities of north-east and north-west Rus'. Defensive thinking tended to be 'one-sided', meaning that the most formidable fortifications were concentrated on one (mainland) side. Instead of raising several rows of defensive military works, these districts focused on building towers and straightening *pryaslos* (sections of wall between towers). As a result, both frontal and flanking fire could be conducted on the mainland side. On the other sides, only frontal fire was still possible, as was typical of earlier fortifications. This arrangement was characteristic of fortresses of the 14th and the first half of the 15th centuries.

The 14th century also brought changes in terminology. While previously a citadel was universally known as a *detinets*, it now retained this name only in a few districts (for example, in Novgorod); in the Moscow and Tver principalities the word *detinets* was replaced by the term *kremlin*, and in Pskov by the word *krom*.

The Zmievy Valy (Snake Ramparts)

In addition to the network of fortresses, continuous ramparts of great length were built to defend against the nomadic warriors. These ramparts can still be seen across the whole of the Ukraine. Surviving sections of these ramparts extend to about 800km, although the original extent was probably 1,000km. Owing to their immense length the ramparts were named Zmievy Valy (Snake Ramparts). With the passage of time the details of by whom and when the ramparts were erected became lost, and succeeding generations believed that such work was beyond the power of humans. A legend thus grew up about a monstrous snake (or a dragon) tamed by the epic blacksmiths Kozma and Demiyan, who harnessed it and forced it to plough the earth. The plough left furrows (the ditches), and the earth raised up by the plough formed the ramparts bordering them. Some even 'saw' the odd-shaped holes at regular intervals beside the ditches and ramparts as marks left by the sharp claws of this mythical snake or dragon.

The ramparts were built in the late 10th and the 11th centuries. Their construction was started under Prince Vladimir and carried on under his successors. The earliest written reference to the ramparts dates from the beginning of the 11th century when Bishop Bruno, visiting Kievan Rus', reported that the Russian prince had protected his state from the nomads with long and formidable fortifications. The Zmievy Valy are mentioned in the Russian annals from the end of the 11th century up to the 13th century. They are sometimes known as the Polovetski Ramparts, which points to their use as defences against the raids of the Polovtsy, the chief enemy of Rus' at that time.

The Zmievy Valy did not form a continuous defensive line, but were part of a complex network. In the most vulnerable places there could be up to seven separate ramparts, and they were raised both along rivers (such as the Dnieper, Ros', Stugna, and Sula) and between them. Natural obstacles, such as the sloping river banks, forests, marshes, etc., were made utmost use of in the construction.

The Zmievy Valy comprised a rampart and a ditch in front of it, on the side of the steppe. Occasionally a ditch ran along both sides of the rampart. Today the ramparts are 2–5m high and about 10m thick. These, however, are average parameters – some parts of the ramparts are as high as 6m and as thick as 25m. The ramparts have inevitably shrunk in the course of time. They are known to have been higher in the mid 19th century, when they reached 6.5m in some places. This certainly suggests that at the time of their construction the Zmievy Valy were higher and steeper. The ramparts were created from the earth dug out from making the ditch, and were sometimes strengthened with clay. Some sections reveal that the rampart was built of sand until it was 2m high and 6m thick, and then provided with a 1.5m-thick layer of clay. After the clay had dried, earth was used to bring the rampart to the required height.

Wooden intra-rampart structures have been discovered inside many ramparts; these allowed a rampart to achieve sufficient height and steepness. These structures consisted of oak log cells, using logs up to 40cm thick, which extended to the top of the rampart creating wooden walls made up of log cells. The walls were relatively short, and probably did not exceed 4m in height as a rule. The overall height of the defences (including the rampart and the wall) was about 10–12m on average, but could vary depending upon the strategic importance of a particular defensive sector.

The Zmievy Valy were closely linked with the fortresses built along the rivers. The ramparts served to contain the enemy's advance until troops arrived from a nearby fortress. Considering that the bulk of the nomadic armies consisted of cavalry, and that they lacked the skills and equipment to assault the fortifications, the ramparts were equal to the task, provided that they were properly manned. Only a state as powerful as Kievan Rus' was capable of providing troops for such extensive fortifications and numerous fortresses into the bargain. When this centralized state disintegrated into separate principalities, the latter proved unable to maintain and defend fortifications of that length. Besides, infighting between principalities now compelled each to defend its own boundaries. The principalities continued to maintain sections of the Zmievy Valy that were vital for their own safety and even raised new ramparts from time to time. For instance, in the second half of the 12th century new ramparts were built in the frontier district between the Chernigov and Pereyaslavl principalities – but these ramparts were neither as high nor as long as the old ones. The changes in the political situation — feudal disunity followed by the Mongol invasion — eventually meant that the Zmievy Valy gradually fell into oblivion.

Design and development

The defences of a Russian *gorod* comprised earthen ramparts, ditches, walls, gates, and towers. Earthen ramparts were the key feature in artificial defensive works in Russia during the period under discussion here. Earlier fortresses either had no or very few towers. Most walls, with the exception of a few districts, were wooden up to the 15th century.

Ramparts

The height of earthen ramparts (*osyp'*) varied greatly depending on the military importance of the fortified settlement. They rarely exceeded 4m, except for in the larger cities, where they could be much higher. For example, the ramparts were about 8m high in Vladimir and 10m in Old Ryazan. The ramparts of 'Yaroslav's city' in Kiev were the most formidable, reaching 16m in height and 25–30m in width at the base.

Ramparts were often built of earth or clay, or more rarely of sand or stone. Sand (being too loose) was only used in districts where earth or clay was unavailable. A rampart built of sand had to be strengthened with a wooden casing. Masonry bonded with earth or lime was extremely rare; where stone was in plentiful supply, it was easier to build a stone wall. Where hard ground was not present, only the front side of the rampart (the face of the slope) was made of it while the rear side was raised with less compact soil. To hamper the enemy attacking a rampart, its front side was often coated with clay and watered.

The top of a rampart consisted of a horizontal strip of ground on which a certain type of wall was erected. Its minimum width – if it served as a base for a palisade – was 1.3m. If the rampart had a log wall on top, the strip was naturally wider – as much as 8 or 9m, especially when it supported a wall made of two rows of log cells. Access to the top of a rampart was granted by wooden ladders or steps cut into the ground. To ensure the uninterrupted movement of the defenders along the rampart during a siege, the rear side of the rampart was paved with stone, or a horizontal terrace was built there. A stepped profile was sometimes given to the entire rear side of the rampart.

12th-century oak logs discovered in the ramparts of Vladimir. Such logs were used to build an intra-rampart structure, giving it its steepness whilst preventing the earth from sliding down. (Historical Museum in Vladimir)

As a rule, a rampart was asymmetrical in cross-section. The front slope was steeper (usually 40–45 degrees, but no less than 30 degrees) than the back one (25–30 degrees). A considerable steepening of the slope on the front side could be attained by the addition of compacted soil or by facing the rampart with stone or wood. However, in Russian fortresses preference was given to intra-rampart structures. Wooden intra-rampart structures are characteristic not only of Russian but of other Slavic fortresses as well, such as Polish and Czech ones. However, although there are some well-known exceptions, Russian intra-rampart structures differed from those found in Poland or the Czech Republic. In general terms,

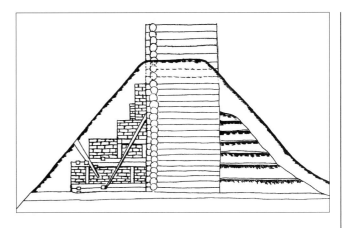

A cutaway view of the rampart of Belgorod. Oak log cells placed close to each other form the base of the rampart. The front wall of the cells was right under the crest of the rampart and found its continuation in a wooden wall on top of it. Facing the cells, in the front part of the rampart there was a wooden framework filled with mud-brick. The rear part of the rampart was strengthened with a layer of clay. The entire intra-rampart structure was covered with earth.

the typical Polish framework consisted of several layers of logs laid perpendicular to each other, the Czech structure consisted of lattice-work and sometimes featured masonry, while the Russians made use of oak-wood log cells packed with earth.

The intra-rampart wooden structure changed with time. The earliest structures of this type were discovered in fortresses built in the late 10th century under Prince Vladimir. The fortifications of Belgorod, Pereyaslavl, and some other cities belong to this type. Structures of this early period are particularly complex. The core of the structure comprised oak-wood log cells placed close to each other so that the front wall of the framework was right under the crest of the rampart. The framework was usually built in such a way that the ends of the logs protruded about 0.5m, and these jutting ends of each shell almost touched those protruding from the next shell. Facing the cells, in the front part of the rampart, a wooden carcass filled with mud-brick bonded with clay was built. Both the carcass and the oak framework were covered with earth. This construction method involved much labour, and was simplified early in the first half of the 11th century when the carcass with mud-brick was dispensed with and only a line of oak cells placed close together was left.

If a rampart was fairly broad, each cell would be long, stretched across the rampart. For extra solidity one or more walls were added, creating several small rooms. For example, the interior of the rampart built in the first half of the 11th century in 'Yaroslav's city' in Kiev reveals oak cells about 19m long (running across the rampart) and 12–16m high. Each cell consists of three long transverse (to the rampart) and seven short longitudinal walls, which, together, divide the cell into 12 rooms. Despite the considerable transverse length of the cells, their facade is located right under the crest of the rampart, as usual.

Intra-rampart log cell structures: the structure consisting of separate log cells discovered in the ramparts of 'Yaroslav's city' in Kiev (left), and a solid structure of log cells (right).

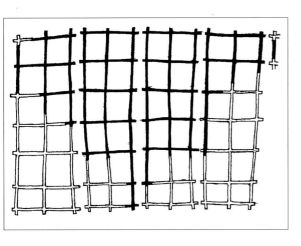

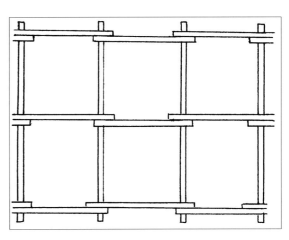

Alongside the structure consisting of separate cells, another structure began to be used as early as the first half of the 11th century. The cells of this structure were consolidated by adding overlapping longitudinal logs. This framework also consisted of several rows of cells. Sometimes only the outside cells were filled with earth whereas the inside cells, overlooking the fortress court, were left hollow. The latter were used as storerooms or living quarters.

Wooden log intra-rampart structures of both types – built of separate cells or forming a continuous line – became widespread in the 11th and 12th centuries, particularly in large cities and strategically important fortresses. However, fortresses defending smaller settlements had purely earthen ramparts with no wooden framework inside. In the centuries that followed there was a tendency to simplify the wooden structures, and by the 13th–15th centuries they consisted usually of no more than a primitive oak log wall with short crossbeams directed to the rear.

Ditches

A ditch was often created in front of a rampart, although it may not always have run along the entire perimeter of the fortifications. For example, in cape layout fortresses the ditch, as a rule, protected the most vulnerable mainland side, cutting the promontory off from the rest of the land; the remaining sides were protected by rivers, deep ravines, and the like.

The earth dug out in the course of making a ditch was used to raise the rampart, so the depth of the ditch generally equalled the height of the adjoining rampart, except when there already was a ravine where the ditch was to be dug, which naturally resulted in the depth of the ditch exceeding the height of the rampart. A ditch usually had a symmetrical profile with walls sloping at 30–45 degrees, with a rounded bottom. Wherever possible, the ditch was filled with water from a river, lake, or other source. When left dry, the bottom of the ditch was filled with sharpened poles. A narrow, horizontal strip of land (or berm) was left between a ditch and a rampart to prevent the rampart sliding into the ditch. These berms were usually about 1m wide.

Walls

There were three main types of fortress walls: palisades (*tyn* or *chastokol*), log walls, and stone walls. The *tyn* was the simplest type, comprising a row of vertical or slightly inclined, sharpened stakes driven into the ground close to each other. This palisade was usually 'two spears high', that is, about 3–4m above ground level. The stakes were driven as deep as 0.5–1m into the ground, and according to archaeological research were 13–18cm thick. About 0.3–0.5m below their pointed ends, the vertical stakes were joined together by a horizontal pole which was either run through special apertures made in the vertical stakes or nailed to them on the outside. On the side of the fortress the palisade was provided with wooden flooring on vertical pillars. This wall-walk for the defenders was called a *polati* or *krovat'*. Sometimes a wall-walk consisted of nothing more than a

Methods of using a *tyn*, and one of the types of fence. A *tyn* could be set up in two rows, one higher than the other, or combined with a log cell structure. A *polati* or *krovat'* – a wall-walk covered with duckboards – was made behind a *tyn*. The *tyn* could have a roof.

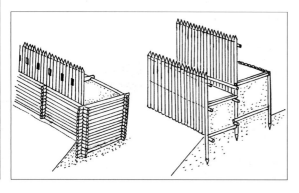

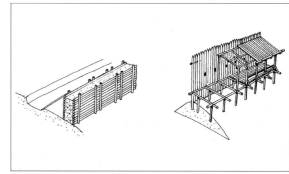

number of short logs driven into the ground, making movement along it much more difficult than on planks.

A *tyn* was not necessarily just a row of stakes. It was sometimes supported to the rear by a small earthen embankment or strengthened from behind with angled logs, whose pointed ends jutted out; two rows of *tyn* might be built (one higher than the other); or a *tyn* could be combined with a log wall. Some examples of *tyn* were roofed. Weapons could be fired either over the top of the *tyn* or through loopholes.

A *tyn* was the only type of wooden fortification in old Slavic settlements in the 8th–9th centuries; later on it provided protection for small settlements and minor fortresses. However, this simple fortification continued to be extensively used even in large cities and strategically important fortresses. It was erected in less vulnerable sectors of defence where the natural relief of the land hampered attack, for example, along riverbanks in cape layout settlements. Moreover, for a long time the *tyn* remained the principal type of fortification of the *okol'ny gorod/possad*. The rather primitive fortifications allocated to these trading areas can be explained by the large areas of land that they occupied. Commercial activities were still closely linked to agriculture, and many citizens were engaged in cattle-breeding and farming. Thus, every homestead had a large plot of land to go with it. Walls of considerable length were difficult to create and hard to defend, and were only meant to protect the inhabitants from wild beasts, gangs of robbers, and nomadic raiders. In times of serious danger the citizens took shelter in the *detinets* and the *okol'ny gorod* was set on fire.

Another type of primitive fortification, the fence, was a rare alternative to the *tyn*. Fences were made of horizontally laid logs squeezed between vertical logs driven into the ground in pairs. The structure of a fence could vary, too; for example, two rows of horizontal logs with earthen filling packed between them could be held in place by vertical ones.

The second half of the 10th century saw the appearance of wooden log walls, created by placing log cells close to each other along the top of a rampart. The cells could have three sides, consisting of a facade stretched along the outer side of the rampart and two transverse walls, or four sides, thus taking on the appearance of a small house. These log cells were called *gorodni*. They were joined by cross-walls but their facades were not joined together (unlike the later *tarassy*-style structure).

The thickness of the log wall varied from 2m to 6m while its height was 3m to 5m. The wall usually had two floors and was covered with a roof. The upper floor had loopholes, but there were no merlons on the wall. A wall-walk (*boevoy hod*) ran behind a parapet supplied with loopholes. The upper part of the wall was built slightly projecting beyond the plane of the wall, so that there was a gap between the upper and lower parts of the wall. The clearance served the same purpose as hoarding or machicolations in European castles: to command the space at the foot of the wall. This overhanging projection is usually called an *oblam* and the entire projecting upper part of the wall the *zaborola*. Disputes, however, continue as to the meaning of the two terms: some consider both terms to be synonymous referring only to the projection, while others assume that *zaborola* stood for the whole of a wall.

Log cell walls were to be found protecting strategically important fortresses, the *detinets* in a large city, or the most crucial sectors of defence in other fortified settlements (such as the mainland side in a settlement situated on a promontory). Sometimes a log wall and a more primitive palisade could be found in different sectors of the same fortress.

Up until the mid 13th century most fortresses had wooden walls. In the Novgorod lands, stone fortresses first appeared as early as the 11th and 12th centuries, although these were exceptions. Stone castles could also be found in this period in Bogolyubovo (built about 1165 in the Suzdal lands) and in Kholm (1237–38, in west Volhynia). Some urban estates and large monasteries also had

Wooden log walls built in the *gorodni* style

Wooden log walls built in the *gorodni* style
This type of structure was the most popular in Rus' between the second half of the 10th and the mid 15th centuries. The upper part of the wall projected slightly forwards as a rule, overhanging the lower part. The resulting clearance, called *oblam*, was designed with the same aim as hoarding or machicolations in European castles – to command the foot of the wall. The wall was usually built on top of an earthen rampart. In order to add steepness to the rampart and prevent the earth from slipping down, intra-rampart structures were often resorted to. These were wooden log cells placed inside the ramparts and usually filled with earth. Occasionally, however, rows of cells on the inner side of the rampart were left empty and used for living in, for household items, and as storerooms.

stone or brick walls – a choice, however, dictated by artistic and ideological considerations above all, as opposed to military necessity. Wooden walls were considered to be perfectly adequate for military purposes, and were built in most fortresses.

Stone defensive walls began to be widely built in the mid 13th century, but even then this was not done all over the country. In some fortresses wooden walls co-existed alongside stone ones. For instance, in the fortress of Velie built in the late 14th–early 15th centuries, one of the walls was stone, 4.4m thick, and the others were made of wood and stood on ramparts. In such timber-and-stone fortresses stone walls were reserved for defending the most vulnerable (usually the mainland) side.

In the 13th–15th centuries the thickness of stone walls varied in different parts of the fortress, reaching 3–4m on the most vulnerable, mainland side while being only 1.5–2m in other places. The walls became thinner towards the top, were crowned with a stone parapet with rectangular merlons, and were usually covered with a gabled wooden roof. The parapet was not less than 55cm thick. The *boevoy hod* (wall-walk) running behind was to be at least 1.5–2m wide to allow two armed warriors to pass each other. Adding the thickness of the parapet to the width of the wall-walk, one can deduce that the minimum width of the top of the wall would have been 2m.

The second half of the 14th century saw a tendency towards increasing the height of stone walls, and from the early 15th century, with the spread of cannon, walls tended to grow in thickness. They were usually 7.5–9m high, although some were higher. External masonry, called *prikladka*, was added to pre-existing stone walls to thicken them. Machicolations and mural galleries with loopholes were not popular features in Russia at that period. In the mid 15th century loopholes began to appear at the foot of walls; however, these were still rare. Fire was

The *boevoy hod* (wall-walk) of Porkhov fortress. In Russian fortresses these were covered with gable roofs, to protect against the weather.

generally effected only through the crenellations of a battlemented parapet. The top of a wall was reached by stairs inside the towers or by ladders fixed to the wall.

Stone walls by no means replaced wooden ones outright. The latter continued to prevail in fortifications. To complicate matters, the wooden walls, unlike stone ones, have not been preserved, which may give the wrong impression as to the scale of their extent. In the 14th and 15th centuries wooden walls were modified due to the development of stone-throwing engines and cannon. They became thicker, consisting not of one but of two or even three rows of logs with earth or rubble filling in between. The most common type of wall now comprised one or two rows of log cells closed on all sides, with their ground floor filled with earth or rubble. This structure had been encountered earlier (from the 10th century onwards) but only became widespread in the 14th–15th centuries.

Gates

Gates in Russian fortresses were placed in gate-towers as a rule. Primitive fortifications might have a gate that was cut out of the wall, much like a common household gate. However, in cities or strategically important fortresses gates were always located in gate-towers. In Rus', no gates have been found in the walls

Two views of the Talavski *zakhab*, Izborsk fortress. This was a narrow passage 36m long and 4m wide. Today the exterior wall of the *zakhab* lies in ruins.

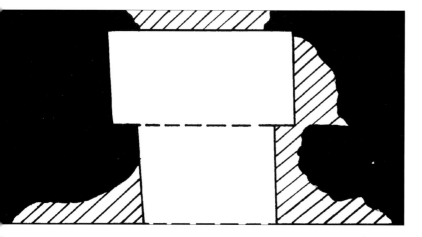

Plan of a *vylaz* (secret exit) in the wall of Izborsk fortress. A *vylaz* was made in a wall to allow sorties. A *vylaz* in a stone wall consisted of a passage inside the wall camouflaged on the exterior with a thin masonry wall that was broken down at the moment a sortie was begun.

Until the very end of the 15th century towers in Russian fortresses narrowed markedly towards the top. For example, the Temnushka Tower in Izborsk fortress, seen here, has a truncated cone in shape. Visible in the foreground are the ruins of the outer wall of the Nikolski *zakhab* that started at this point.

between two flanking towers, with the exception of the late Kopor'e fortress, which was probably built with the participation of foreign craftsmen.

In the 10th–12th centuries gate-towers were the only towers in a fortress, with the exception of watchtowers, which were rare. The gate in a gate-tower was placed on the same level as the rampart's base, so the tower itself, sitting considerably below the walls, looked as if it was cut into the rampart, and barely rose above the walls. Nor was the tower designed for flanking fire, leading many researchers to consider it an unusual form of a gate rather than a tower, and that in fortresses of the period there were no towers whatsoever. It should be noted that chroniclers are of the same opinion: gate-towers were merely called gates, not towers.

These gate-towers were mostly made of wood and covered with hip roofs (i.e. roofs with four or more sloping sides). It was only in the large cities like Kiev or Vladimir that gate-towers were made of stone or brick. Here, in addition to their military function, they served as triumphal arches symbolizing the wealth and greatness of the city, and were often embellished with decorations. In Kievan Rus' a tradition began of accommodating a small chapel in gate-towers, which served no defensive function; or sometimes an icon was placed above the gate instead. Chapels and icons were believed to secure 'heavenly protection' for the town. This tradition survived in Russian fortifications until quite recently, such as in the Siberian *ostrogs* of the 18th–19th centuries.

Interior view of the Malaya Tower of Porkhov fortress. The exit onto the walls here is on the rear side of the tower, on the level of the wall-walk. There would be a temporary wooden platform here, which could be easily destroyed in the event that the enemy seized the wall.

While prior to the 14th century the gate was usually placed on the mainland side, after this it was built on one of the sides less vulnerable to attack. The gateway in earlier fortresses, and later on in minor ones, ran perpendicular to the rampart. From the 12th century onwards, however, parts of the rampart flanking the entrance were sometimes shifted, so that the gateway ran parallel to the ramparts. As a result the enemy would find themselves trapped in a narrow passage between the ramparts. In the 14th and 15th centuries this idea developed into an intricate gate complex called a *zakhab*. This was a long, narrow, often winding corridor between walls, where the enemy found themselves under cross-fire. The *zakhab* usually had two gates: one at the entrance and the other at the exit from the corridor, with the outer gate at a right angle to the inner one where possible. In many cases the *zakhab* was additionally strengthened with

Loopholes in the Vyshka Tower. This was one of the four circular towers of Izborsk fortress, which were built in the late 14th century and modernized in the early 15th and then early 16th centuries. The loopholes are clearly arranged not one above the other but in a 'chessboard' fashion, to eliminate dead ground. On the left, between the storeys, are three square sockets left by the beams of the ceiling.

tower placed next to the outer gate, or above one of the gates, or in the middle of the *zakhab* corridor. *Zakhabs* could be present in both stone and wooden fortresses. The remains of stone ones can be found at Izborsk, Ostrov, Porkhov and Pskov.

From the 14th century onwards gates were provided with portcullises, usually made of iron although examples survive of wooden ones with iron facings.

In some fortresses there were also secret exits (*vylaz*) used by the defenders to make surprise sorties. The *vylaz* in a timber-and-earth fortress took the form of a boarded tunnel built through a rampart with a disguised exit on the outside. In a stone fortress, they took the form of a passage in the wall with the exit concealed behind a thin layer of masonry. The masonry could be easily smashed through to make a sortie and then replaced later. The remains of *vylaz* can be seen in the fortresses of Izborsk and Porkhov.

A bridge in front of a gate was usually narrow, and built on permanent pillars. Up to the 15th century all bridges were wooden and could easily be destroyed following news of the approaching enemy. A bridge could sometimes be turned into a trap as, for example, in 1426 in Opochki, where the defenders let the assailants seize the bridge only to bring it crashing down into a ditch filled with sharpened stakes. The mid 15th century saw the first stone bridges built in Rus', and at the end of the 15th century drawbridges first began to appear.

Towers

Up to the mid 13th century there were practically no towers in Russian fortresses apart from the gate-tower, and one or two other towers at most. The second half of the 13th century saw a growth of free-standing towers in the fortresses of the Galich-Volhynia principality, which came under the influence of its western neighbours Poland and Hungary. These towers were placed inside the walls and near to the side of the fortress most vulnerable to attack. They served concurrently as watchtowers, a second line of defence allowing fire to be brought to bear upon the assailants, as points for directing defensive operations, and as the place of final refuge if the enemy broke into the fortress. While all the other fortifications were wooden, these donjons were often built of stone or brick. Examples still survive at Berestie, Kamenets, Stolpie, and Czartoryisk. The tower in Berestie was virtually square at the base (5.9m × 6.3m) with walls 1.3m thick. Kamenets has a circular brick tower 29.4m high, 13.5m in diameter, and with 2.5m-thick walls. In Stolpie the tower is of stone, 20m high, and rectangular on the outside (5.8m × 6.3m) but circular inside (about 3m in diameter). The round tower in Czartoryisk greatly resembles that of Kamenets.

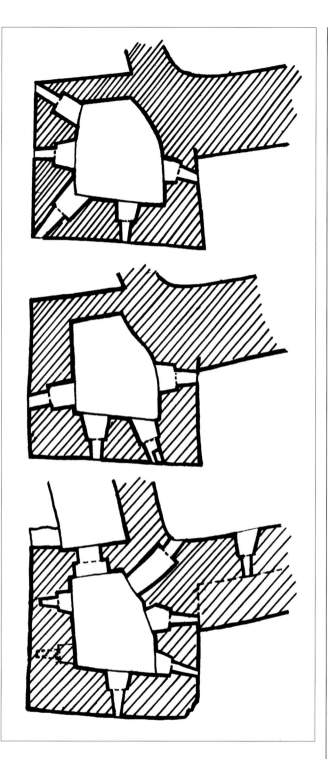

The arrangement of loopholes in the ground, first, and second storeys (tiers) of the Talavskaya Tower in Izborsk fortress. Note that the arrangement of the loopholes is not repeated. They all face different directions, thus commanding every area in front of the tower.

Ways of joining log ends: 'v oblo' (A) and 'v lapu' (B). The first way, with log ends sticking out, was more popular in log cell walls, while in wooden towers both ways were used. The 'v lapu' way was preferred in polyhedral towers as it facilitated the joining of logs at angles greater than 90 degrees.

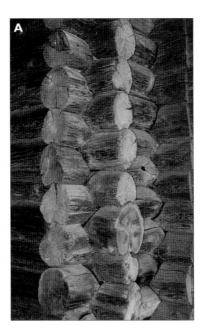

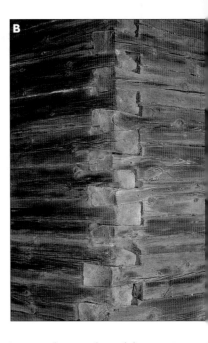

A fragment of an oak tower of the Moscow Kremlin of 1339–40 and the method of joining logs in it. The logs are joined 'v lapu', that is with their ends not sticking out. Special grooves and projections were made at the intersections to provide greater strength (they can clearly be seen in the right-hand illustration). The angle between the logs is 135 degrees, which indicates that the tower was octagonal. (Historical Museum in Moscow)

The 14th and especially 15th centuries saw the number of fortress towers increase rapidly, and they now played an active part in the defence. They were extended beyond the line of the walls to allow flanking fire along the adjoining curtain walls. The increased use of cannon enhanced their importance, as it was here, and not on the walls, that cannon were originally mounted. Towers were still usually sited on the most vulnerable, mainland side.

Stone towers could be rectangular, circular, or semi-circular (known as *persi*), while wooden towers were rectangular or polygonal (hexagonal or octagonal). Circular and semi-circular stone towers are supposed to have been better suited to conducting sweeping fire and better at withstanding direct hits than rectangular ones, whose corners were easily damaged. Nevertheless, from the 14th and 15th centuries onwards even newly built fortresses were still provided with rectangular towers alongside circular and semi-circular ones. Although the latter became more numerous, they did not fully replace the former, which is evidence of certain advantages held by rectangular towers. It is interesting to note that even in a single fortress towers were never identical; their height and footprints differed widely.

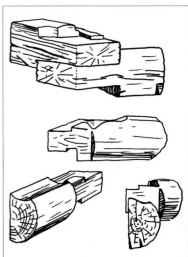

One of the walls in Gdov fortress, made of alternating horizontal layers of two sorts of stone (boulders and limestone).

Towers dating from the 13th to 15th centuries are narrower towards the top. Moreover, their walls are sometimes slightly curved so that they often resemble inverted cauldrons.

Rectangular towers in Rus' were never built open on the inside (i.e. three-sided). Only semi-circular towers were open. Both open and closed towers had their own specific advantages. Open ones allowed the defenders in the citadel or donjon to shoot any soldiers who turned traitor inside the towers, or to easily push the enemy out of an occupied tower. On the other hand, a closed tower could be turned into an independent centre of resistance in case the enemy seized part of the fortifications. In Rus' preference was given to the closed tower.

Both wooden and stone towers were multi-tiered. The number of storeys varied from two to six but usually was three or four (including the ground floor). The storeys had beamed ceilings and the holes for the beams can still be seen in stone towers. Movement between the floors was via wooden stairs or sometimes ladders; the latter were pulled up in times of danger. As a rule, the upper floor of wooden towers had an overhanging projection (*oblam*), which allowed fire to be brought to bear on the enemy at the foot of the tower. Towers had wooden hip roofs. The lower part of the roof usually had a gently sloping pitch conducive to draining water off the tower walls. Hip roofs on towers were often topped with a watchtower (sometimes equipped with a bell) where a sentinel could keep watch. This watchtower was, in its turn, covered with a smaller hip roof, itself crowned with a weathervane. Towers open on the top were extremely rare.

A wall-walk (*boevoy hod*) ran through one of the storeys of the tower, usually with two doors allowing access to it – although from the point of view of defence this was not ideal, as a wooden door was easy enough to destroy. An improvement to this was an exit on the rear side of the tower leading to a small wooden platform connected to the *boevoy hod* on the walls. The platform was temporary and could be quickly destroyed, considerably hampering the enemy.

Towers could be called *stolp, vezha, kostyor,* or *strel'nitsa*. A *stolp* was a tower not connected with the fortress walls but was free-standing, as per the donjons in the Volhynia fortresses. A tower was called a *kostyor* in the Pskov and Novgorod lands and a *strel'nitsa* in the Moscow district. *Vezha* was a general, commonly used term. The word *bashnya* replaced all these terms in the 16th century and has remained in use ever since.

Decorations on the Vyshka Tower and the adjoining wall, Izborsk fortress. Various kinds of crosses and elegant designs as well as round rosettes were characteristic elements of Russian fortification decor.

All the storeys of a tower (often including the ground floor) were provided with rectangular loopholes, both narrow (for arrow shot) and wide (for cannon); in contrast, loopholes were rare in walls in the period under discussion. Tower loopholes were arranged fan-shaped, with loopholes in different storeys facing different directions, aimed at eliminating dead space. The 14th century saw some loopholes with box-rooms on the inside, however these did not become widespread until the 15th century when *pechuras*, as they were known, began to be used for cannon. Disguised loopholes, concealed behind masonry on the outside, are today rare and unlike those blocked up later they were created at the time of the tower's construction. Disguised loopholes were probably designed to surprise the enemy; the thin front wall could be easily broken down and fire brought to bear on the enemy at an unexpected angle.

Methods of construction

Logs in wooden cell walls were generally joined 'v oblo', that is with the ends of the logs sticking out. This method was used alongside the 'v lapu' method without the ends sticking out. The latter was particularly suitable for polygonal towers where the angle between logs was over 90 degrees. This method of joining logs can be seen on a discovered fragment of a tower of the Moscow Kremlin built of oak wood in 1339–40. The angle between the logs is 135 degrees here which allows us to assume that the tower was octagonal. The logs featured special grooves and notches where they were joined together, making a very solid structure. With an intra-rampart framework, the wooden wall was usually its extension. Otherwise, a wall was generally erected on piles driven into the rampart.

Stone walls were laid with clay or mortar, never dry stone. The structure of the wall resembled a sandwich, with a layer of soft or crushed stone mixed with mortar placed between two layers of hard stone. Monolithic construction methods were much rarer. Some stone walls had a stratified structure, consisting of horizontal rows of various kinds of stone. The walls of Gdov fortress offer a vivid example of this, with rows of boulders alternating with rows of limestone. The walls and towers of stone fortresses often featured symbolic crosses, elegant girdles laid in triangles or diamonds, and round rosettes.

A tour of the sites

Most Russian fortifications dating from this period were made of timber and earth, of which only the grass-covered ramparts remain. Impressive examples of fortifications only survive in north-west Russia where masonry was widely used. The four sites examined below are two border fortresses (Izborsk and Porkhov), Pskov, and Truvor's *gorodishche*. Izborsk was a strategically important outpost near Pskov at the Russian frontier with Livonian and German lands. Porkhov was one of Novgorod's frontier fortresses. Pskov, the capital of an independent principality, is an example of a stone citadel and urban fortifications, whereas Truvor's *gorodishche* gives an idea of what an old timber-and-earth fortress town looked like.

Truvor's *gorodishche* and Izborsk fortress

The fortress of Izborsk lies 30km west of Pskov, and nearby is the site of an earlier fortification, Truvor's *gorodishche*. Although the latter was first mentioned in the annals of 862, a settlement existed there as far back as the turn of the 7th/8th century. The 10th and 11th centuries saw the settlement double in size and occupying the entire promontory surrounded by deep, steep-sloped ravines. A rampart was erected on the most vulnerable, mainland side and a ditch dug out in front of it. The entire settlement was enclosed within a wall of oakwood. By the 12th century the fortifications of the settlement had been modified again. The height of the rampart was increased to 6m. The wooden wall along the perimeter was replaced by a stone one 3m thick and 3m high. On top of this stone foundation there was probably a wooden log wall with a wall-walk. A stone hexagonal tower with 1.5m-thick walls was erected on the tip of the promontory, between the ravines – the only tower in the fortress. It had a postern gate to one side, allowing the defenders to make sorties. This secret exit was blocked with a stone on the outside, and was only 0.8m wide and 1m high. Two gates led into the fortress, the western giving access to the trading area (*possad*) and the eastern leading to the lake where there must have been a landing point and a market place.

The size of the fortress was limited by the size of the promontory on which it lay. Therefore, in 1303 Izborsk was transferred to another site, half a kilometre to the south of the *gorodishche*. At first, this new settlement had wooden walls and a circular stone tower (the Lukovka) 13m high and 9.5m in diameter. Like that of the earlier Truvor's *gorodishche*, this single tower was placed on the tip of the promontory. In 1330, when the wooden walls were replaced by stone ones, the Lukovka was surrounded with external walls, thus turning it into a donjon. The

BOTH The rampart and a reconstruction of the gate in Truvor's *gorodishche*. The gate is on one side of the rampart and the road leading to it ran between the rampart and a precipice. Flanking the gate are the remains of a stone layer that was once 3m thick and 3m high and served as a base for a wooden wall.

The Lukovka Tower, Izborsk fortress. Built in 1303, it was the only stone tower in the fortress at this date; all the other fortifications were still wooden. In the course of the modernization of the fortress in 1330 the wooden walls were replaced with stone ones and the Lukovka Tower found itself inside the fortress walls, becoming a donjon.

tower was used as an armoury and served as a watch and signal tower as well. At the end of the 14th century the fortress walls were supplied with six more towers — four circular and two rectangular (one of the latter has not been preserved). At the beginning of the 15th and then early in the 16th centuries the fortifications were modernized: the walls became thicker and the towers were adapted for use with cannon. As a result, the thickness of the walls on the most vulnerable side reaches 5m while on the other sides the walls are 2.5–3.7m thick. The towers are concentrated where the danger was greatest, and the distance between them does not exceed 60m. Protruding far beyond the wall line, they allow effective flanking fire to be brought to bear upon the enemy. Two entrances led to the fortress, each provided with a *zakhab* (barbican). The Nikolski *zakhab* was 90m long and 5m wide while the Talavski *zakhab* was 36m long and 4m wide. In the 17th century the inner gate of the Nikolski *zakhab* was fitted with a tower with a portcullis. The south-east side of the fortress had a *tainik* – an underground, masonry-lined corridor leading to a spring well. Up to the 16th century Izborsk fortress survived eight serious sieges and never surrendered. It only fell in 1569 through treachery and was later captured by the troops of Stephen Batory in 1581.

Today all that remains of Truvor's *gorodishche* is a rampart, a ditch, and some fragments of stone walling. The stone fortress of Izborsk is well preserved, except for the Nikolski *zakhab* and two towers, which lie in ruin. Decorative crosses and other ornaments can be seen on the walls and towers of the fortress.

Porkhov fortress

Situated 75km east of Pskov, Porkhov fortress was a powerful outpost of the Novgorodians. The fortress was founded in 1239 on the banks of the River Shelon. Its defences consisted of two lines of ramparts and ditches. A wooden log wall ran along the top of the main rampart. Between 1300 and 1387 the fortifications were twice modernized: they were raised in height and the slopes of the ramparts became steeper. At the same time a stone foundation 0.7m high and 3.5m thick was built to underpin the wooden wall on the rampart. Nevertheless, by the late 14th century the fortress could no longer provide a sufficient defence of the area, and in 1387 it was abandoned and a new fortress was founded. The latter was built on an island further down the Shelon, 1,300m from the old fortress. The fortress walls built of stone and mortar were 8.8m high and nearly 2m thick, and were crowned with broad rectangular merlons. As the walls followed the contours of the island, the fortress took the shape of an irregular pentagon. It had only three towers, placed in the most vulnerable section. Here the curtains between the towers were straight, providing for flanking fire. The builders considered the western wall sufficiently protected by the river and no towers were erected there; moreover, the wall itself was not straight but followed the limits of the island.

The Malaya (Small) Tower was so called because it was the smallest in height and had the fewest loopholes (16); it had five storeys (including the ground floor). Because the ground in front of it was swampy, only a small tower was deemed necessary. It is curious that the Malaya Tower was not provided with a through-passage on the wall-walk level. One could only get out onto the walls from the butt-end of the tower where there was a removable platform. The Nikolskaya Tower was considerably more formidable. It barred the main entrance to the fortress through the so-called Nikolski *zakhab* – a passage 21.5m long and 5m wide running between the walls. The Nikolskaya Tower was 17.3m high and was about twice the height of the walls. It had six storeys (including the ground floor) and 27 loopholes, and permitted firing in all directions from the two upper storeys. Its walls at ground level were 2.6m thick, twice as thick as the walls of the Malaya Tower. However, the most formidable was the Srednyaya (Middle) Tower, which was the same height and had the same number of storeys as the Nikolskaya Tower but had 30 loopholes. It is the only semi-circular tower in the fortress, the others being rectangular.

In addition to the entrance through the Nikolski *zakhab* there was another entrance also defended by a *zakhab*. The latter, known as the Pskovski *zakhab*, was a 35m-long passage leading between two parallel walls each 2.5m thick. The enemy would come under fire along the entire passage through the loopholes in the wall. A 20m-long underground *tainik* leading to the river supplied the fortress with water.

The Srednyaya Tower of Porkhov fortress. There is an awning over it to shelter the restorers from the weather. Like other towers in Russian fortresses, this one had a wooden hip roof. The adjacent *pryaslos* (curtain walls) are missing their upper part, which probably comprised a battlemented parapet with a wooden roof over it.

The *krom* (citadel) in Pskov, viewed from a bridge across the River Velikaya. The famous rampart, the Persi, is between the two towers on the right.

The Persi rampart, which protected the Pskov *krom* on the most vulnerable, mainland side. The Persi was first mentioned in the annals of 1065 but already existed in the 9th–10th centuries. It was modernized several times prior to the 19th century.

Porkhov was built in 1387 when gunpowder artillery was not yet widespread in Rus'. The fortress was thus not suitable for cannon, nor could its rather thin walls withstand fire from heavy bombardment. All these shortcomings were quickly brought to light during the siege laid by the Lithuanians in 1427–28, where the fortress had to pay the attackers off. In 1430 the Novgorodians set about rebuilding the heavily damaged fortress. The thickness of the walls at all vulnerable sectors was increased to 5m at the base. Only the Malaya Tower and the adjacent curtains retained their 14th-century appearance. The loopholes were adjusted for the use of firearms; the fortress overall had 36 loopholes for cannon and about 250 for handheld firearms. Porkhov became one of the first fortresses in northern Rus' to be adapted for cannon.

About the mid 15th century both the *zakhabs* of the fortress were improved. A wall with a gate was built in front of the Nikolskaya Tower. As a result, the main entrance turned into an intricate defensive complex: now the enemy had to first seize the passage through the Tainichnye Gate with its drawbridge and two portcullises, then the new *zakhab* between this gate and the gate in the Nikolskaya Tower, then the old *zakhab*, and finally the last gate in the main wall of the fortress. The Pskovski *zakhab* was provided with the Pskovskaya Tower, which became the second D-shaped tower in the fortress. It had 6 storeys (including the ground floor) and was equipped with 15 loopholes for cannon and 11 for handheld firearms. The fortress was now well equipped for defence on the most vulnerable southern and eastern sides; here the towers projected beyond the line of the walls and the curtains were straight. As for the western side, with its winding walls and lack of machicolations and flanking towers, it remained weak from a defensive point of view, since it allowed the enemy a place

of relative safety at the foot of the wall. Only one loophole for cannon providing for fire to be brought to bear upon the opposite side of the River Shelon was made on this side between 1445 and 1475.

In 1665 the crumbling *tainik* was replaced with a new one, built under the *zakhab* by the Nikolskaya Tower; soon, however, it began to crumble too. Towards the end of the 17th century the fortress lost its military significance, and its defences thereafter have never been modernized. A bell-tower was constructed on top of the Nikolskaya Tower in the 18th century. The fortifications are decorated with crosses: the large one on the wall facing the River Shelon was laid as early as 1387, while the four smaller crosses appeared on the Srednyaya Tower and the adjusting walls following the modernization of the 1430s. The fortifications have been well preserved with the exception of both *zakhabs* and the Pskovskaya Tower, which lie in ruins.

Pskov

Pskov was first mentioned in the annals of 903. The old town was situated on a promontory at the confluence of two rivers – the Pskova and the Velikaya. The fortifications of the 10th century consisted of an earthen rampart topped with a palisade. On its most vulnerable, southern, mainland side the promontory was protected with a moat connecting the two rivers. The moat had been cut in the rock and the extracted stone was used for facing the rampart that stretched along the inward side of the moat. The formidable rampart was a subject of pride to the citizens and the most important part of the defence; it was called the Persi, which means 'breast' in Slav. Although the Persi was first mentioned in the annals of 1065, it already existed as early as the 10th and possibly 9th centuries. In 1192 the Persi was rebuilt; at its ends two gates with *zakhabs* were built. This is the first mention of this kind of construction, which did not become popular until the 14th–15th centuries. The fortifications of Pskov were next modernized in the 14th century when the Livonian Order intensified its onslaught on the city. That century alone saw as many as four sieges laid to Pskov by the Livonian knights. In view of this, the Persi was rebuilt in 1337 and then again in 1394. In the course of the second reconstruction a municipal bell-tower was erected in the centre of the bow-shaped rampart. However, in 1427 a 50m section of the Persi together with the bell-tower fell into the ditch. The same year saw the Persi rebuilt and topped with wooden walls and a new bell-tower. The next wide-scale redevelopment was undertaken in 1466 when the Persi was fortified with three buttresses; a battlemented parapet ran along its top. The Persi still looks impressive today, despite the passing of five centuries. Early in the 18th century the crumbling bell-tower was pulled down, which resulted in the Persi taking on

The gate of the Pskov *krom* (citadel) and a *zakhab* beyond it. The right-hand photograph was taken very near to the gate. Here the *zakhab* begins – a long, winding passage commanded on both sides by the occupants (note the surviving loopholes in the right-hand wall). The *zakhab* ended with a second, inner gate that has not been preserved.

The Kutekroma Tower viewed from the inside of the fortress, the Pskov *krom* (citadel). The tower was built on the very tip of the promontory in 1400.

a somewhat simplified appearance. The second half of the 19th century saw a 'European'-style polyhedral tower erected on the western extremity of the Persi, where an earlier tower used to stand. The Persi itself has dropped at least 5–6m into the ground. Nevertheless, even today the gate in the Persi rampart opens into an impressive *zakhab* – a long, winding corridor exposed to fire from walls and towers and leading to the inner gate, which does not survive.

In 1266 Prince Dovmont built another stone wall, south of the Persi, and in 1377 it was strengthened with two towers. The space between this wall and the Persi was later called 'Dovmont's city' and housed the prince's court and numerous churches. The walls of the town were redeveloped in the 15th century and only a fragment of them has been preserved on the western side. Another stone wall was raised in 1309 on the southern side between the rivers Velikaya and Pskova. Earthen ramparts topped with a comparatively low palisade ran parallel to the rivers from this wall to the wall of 'Dovmont's city'; by 1320 these ramparts were also built of stone. Towers and gates were dotted along the 3.5m-thick stone walls. These stone fortifications protected a considerable part of the trading area (*possad*). However by 1375 the *possad* had already expanded to such an extent that the necessity of building new defensive walls became apparent. From 1375 to 1380 the wooden wall protecting the suburb was replaced by a new, fourth, stone wall on the southern side. The wall was 5m thick at the base and was strengthened with nine towers (*kostyors*), of which only a single tower (the Mstislavskaya) survives to this day. To build this new wall, the wall of 1309 was dismantled.

With the exception of the mainland side, the fortifications of the Pskov citadel (*detinets* or *krom*) remained timber and earth up to the end of the 14th century. In 1400 stone was used to build a wall along the River Velikaya as well as two towers: one (Kutekroma) on the very edge of the promontory and the other nearer to the Persi. The wall along the River Pskova remained wooden. In 1417 a stone tower (the Srednyaya) was erected on it, but a few years later the tower collapsed and had to be rebuilt. In 1419 the tower was connected to the Persi with a stone wall, which shortly afterwards collapsed due to poor foundations. Another wooden wall replaced it. It was not until 1452 that the entire eastern wall of the *krom* was built in stone. In the 16th century the walls along the River Velikaya grew in thickness and height. At the same time the Ploskaya (Flat) Tower was connected to the Kutekroma Tower by a wall on the very tip of the promontory. The fortifications of the Pskov citadel have been beautifully restored and today are very impressive.

In 1465 Pskov found itself enclosed in three lines of stone walls featuring some 20 towers. In 1465–67 the threat of invasion made the authorities encircle the furthest settlements with wooden walls, including those on the other bank of the River Pskova. In 1481 these wooden fortifications were replaced by stone. In the 16th century all the fortifications of the *possad* became stone. Many towers and large sections of the walls of these urban fortifications survive to this day.

The living sites

The largest part of any city was taken up by the *dvors* – the estates of princes, boyars, and bishops, and the courtyards of common freeborn citizens. Each *dvor* was separated from the streets and from neighbouring *dvors* with fences, which were frequently palisades, made of vertical logs 2–2.5m high. It is interesting to note that the boundaries of these *dvors* remained unchanged for long periods of time. For instance, some *dvors* discovered in Novgorod did not change their boundaries from the mid-10th to the mid-15th centuries. Each *dvor* was not divided among all the children of a deceased owner, rather it was inherited by one child alone. On the one hand, the ownership of a *dvor* must have placed the owner under certain obligations (paying taxes, building fortifications, paving streets, participating in the defence of the city, etc.); on the other hand, it qualified him to take part in local government. As these rights and obligations were difficult, sometimes impossible, to differentiate, it was considered best to leave the boundaries of city *dvors* unchanged in Rus'.

Dvors differed in size, depending on the income of the owner. Feudal lords owned estates whose size varied from one city to another. For instance, in Novgorod they were between 1,200–2,000m^2 while in minor towns they were usually smaller. In feudal lords' estates archaeologists have discovered up to a dozen and a half dwellings and outbuildings, such as the owner's house, servants' quarters, barns, bathhouses, and even craftsmen's shops. The buildings often stood around the perimeter of the fence, though sometimes they were put in the centre of the yard. Although their outward boundaries remained intact, these estates could be partitioned into several sites. Wealthy feudal families had several *dvors*, and they were usually grouped in one part of a city or in one street, creating a kind of clan area.

The courtyards of common freeborn citizens were not only smaller (400–460m^2 in Novgorod and 300–800m^2 in Kiev) but were of regular size. They were rectangular, and as a rule were of the same length and width. They seem to have been measured and apportioned by someone simultaneously according to a pre-arranged plan. A dwelling house was generally placed in the corner farthest from the entrance while two or three outbuildings (barns, cattle-sheds, or bathhouses) were to be found on the other side of the yard.

Churches and a market place were key features of a city. The larger cities had dozens of the former, and Novgorod is known to have lost 15 churches in the fire in 1211. Churches were practically the first urban structures to be raised in stone or brick. Masonry churches were already numerous when urban fortifications and all the houses were still wooden. The Desyatinnaya church in Kiev was built back in the late 10th century and the famous St Sophia's cathedral dates from the beginning of the 11th century. One or several churches were usually put close to the market place to pacify the malcontents who frequently gathered there. The churches were also used for the upkeep of trading standards.

The social make up of city districts varied from one town to another. The residences of both the prince and bishop were, as a rule, situated in the *detinets* (citadel); however, there were cities where the *detinets* only housed the

Three lines of ramparts and ditches protected a settlement near the modern village of Poyarkovo. Wooden walls stood on top of the ramparts. Gate-towers once sat in the ramparts where we now see only gaps.

The Cathedral of St Dmitri in Vladimir, erected in 1193–97 inside the *detinets* (citadel). This prince's court cathedral was decorated with intricate stone carvings.

prince's (Kiev) or the bishop's (Novgorod, Smolensk) residence. No clear-cut division existed in the *possad* between quarters occupied by the nobility and the commoners. For instance, the principal part of Kiev, Verkhni Gorod (Upper Town), which comprised 'Vladimir's city', 'Yaroslav's city' and 'Izyaslav's city', was populated not only by the 'upper crust' (the boyars' and prince's families), but also by merchants and craftsmen; there was a Jewish quarter here too. Boyars' estates have been discovered in all the quarters of the *possad* in Novgorod, and in Galich a number of them lay even beyond the line of the city fortifications. Significantly, not a single case is known of princes or boyars hiding themselves from their rebellious subjects behind the walls of a *detinets*. When revolts did take place, the princes and boyars would try to flee the city, but did not seek refuge in the *detinets*. Thus, the *detinets* was never used in opposition to the rest of the city.

Dwellings were of two types: over-ground ones and so-called semi-dugouts. The latter were more popular than the former until the late 11th century, and were widespread in the 9th to the mid 10th century in the forest-steppe; they could also be found further to the south in the steppe, and to the north in the forested areas. In other words, they represented the main type of dwelling in the basins of the Dniester, Dnieper, Oka and Don rivers. It was only in the capital city of Kiev that both types of dwellings co-existed. Unlike the southern districts, the northern Russian (Novgorod and Pskov) lands rarely contained any semi-dugouts. Little by little over-ground dwellings began to appear further south, halfway through the forested zone. The second half of the 10th and 11th centuries saw them in the territory of modern Belarus and in the Ryazan lands alongside semi-dugouts. In the 12th century and after, over-ground dwellings were being built almost everywhere. Whilst omnipresent in the north, they co-existed with semi-dugouts in the western (Galich and Volhynia) and eastern (the Oka basin) lands; only in the mid-Dnieper districts of Kiev, Pereyaslavl, and others did semi-dugouts still predominate.

Semi-dugouts were rectangular houses, almost square in plan, dug on average 0.5–1m into the ground. They differed from over-ground dwellings in that their earthen floor was below ground level; most of a semi-dugout house towered above

OPPOSITE **Zakhabs, a tainik and a tainichnaya bashnya**
In the 14th and 15th centuries *zakhabs* became widespread in Russian fortresses, both stone and wooden. This ante-gate fortification was a long, narrow, often winding passage between two walls, which the enemy had to pass through under crossfire. A *zakhab* was usually provided with two gates – at the entrance and at the exit, with the outer gate at an angle to the inner one if possible – though there were *zakhabs* with only one, inner gate. A *zakhab* was frequently strengthened with a tower placed by the outer gate, or over one of the gates, or in the middle of the passage. This illustration shows three *zakhabs* of the late 15th century: the Talavski (**1**) and Nikolski (**2**) *zakhabs* of Izborsk fortress (after V. V. Kostochkin), and the Nikolski Zakhab (**3**) of Porkhov fortress (after E. G. Arapova and A. N. Kirpichnikov).

There were different ways of supplying a fortress with water: it could be stored in barrels, or wells could be dug inside the fortress if no natural sources were found, or the fortress itself could be built right on the bend of a river or channel. Natural sources and wells were the safest means as they tended not to run dry and it was practically impossible to drain them. However, natural sources were not always available and it was not always possible to dig a well. Therefore, in Rus' they often resorted to the building of a *tainik* (**4**), a secret underground passage going down the slope of a hill towards a river, a natural source, or a place where a well could be easily dug out. Until the late 15th century the entrance to a *tainik* was situated close to the fortress wall; later on it was made in the tower closest to the river. The tower then took on the name of *tainichnaya* (or *tainitskaya*) *bashnya* (**5**).

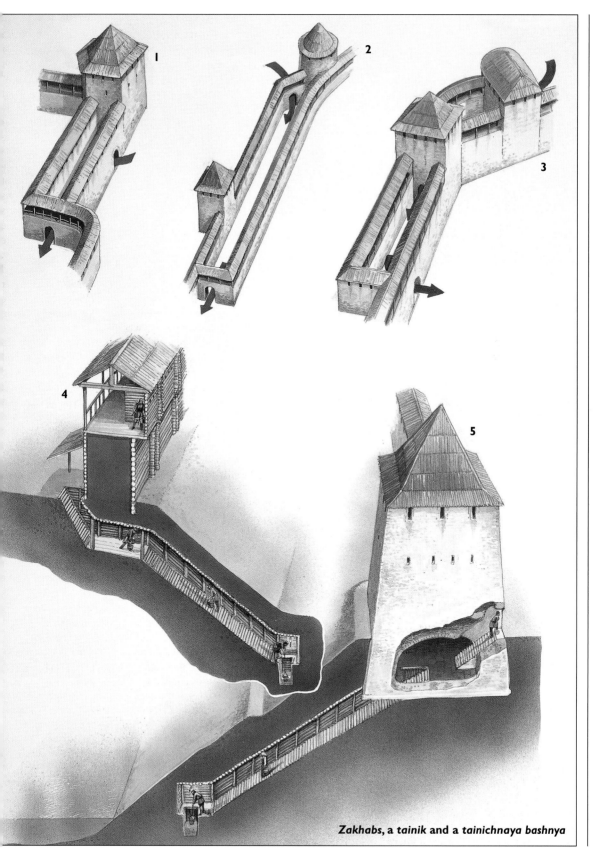

Zakhabs, a tainik and a *tainichnaya bashnya*

The rampart of Yuriev-Polski, built in the 12th century. The roughly 1km-long rampart surrounded a settlement that was almost circular in plan. As usual, the rampart was topped with wooden walls. The roofs of a later monastery are visible beyond the rampart.

the ground though. The walls were made of wood and could be constructed in two ways: from logs whose ends were joined together, or from logs or boards that were laid between vertical poles. Houses of both types are sometimes discovered in one and the same settlement. On the whole, however, in the 9th to the mid 10th centuries log-structure dwellings were more characteristic of the districts west of the Dnieper, while pole-structure dwellings prevailed to its east. With time, the latter came to dominate everywhere. The length and the width of a semi-dugout house varied from 2.3 to 5.5m but were usually 3.0 to 4.5m. The entrance to a semi-dugout house of the 9th–11th centuries was on the southern side as a rule; there were probably no windows at that time so the doorway was the only source of daylight. In the 12th and 13th centuries the entrance was no longer strictly oriented to the south, which must have been connected with the appearance of windows. The floor was left as earth or covered with clay. Semi-dugouts had a wooden, clay-daubed, roof; gambrel roofs (two-sided with a double slope on each side) were probably common too.

Over-ground dwellings were rectangular, sometimes square, houses with sides 4.5–5m long. Their walls consisted of horizontally placed logs joined '*v oblo*' (with ends sticking out) at the corners. Any gaps between the logs were filled with moss. In some areas the walls were clay-daubed, in others they were left wooden. The floor consisted of planks.

Early dwellings had only one room. In the 10th and 11th centuries the room was partitioned into two chambers, and the 12th century saw the appearance of dwellings that consisted of several rooms. In a two-room house the smaller room was on the side of the entrance. The size of multi-room structures varied from 3m to 6m in width and 8m to 9m in length. Multi-room dwellings, undoubtedly belonging to the most wealthy, date back to the 12th–14th centuries. One might think that they would have appeared a little earlier, along with the formation of a class structure of society, but archeological research has shown that a large-scale social differentiation in dwellings was not apparent until the 12th century. Nor were houses of one or more storeys above the ground floor built until the 12th–13th centuries. Dwellings consisting only of a ground floor remained characteristic of Rus' throughout the Middle Ages.

One more type of building is worthy of attention. Twenty-six out of 1,306 *gorodishches* dating from the 10th–13th centuries reveal wooden cells structurally connected with the base of the defensive ramparts. These cells constituted one row (very occasionally two rows) of rooms, 7.5–13.5m^2 in size, which stretched out parallel to the rampart on its inner side. They were sometimes independent log cells placed close to each other, but more often they were joined in a system. A larger cell could be found next to a smaller one, and it was often the latter that housed an oven. There is evidence of a two-chamber structure in some dwellings. The cells were as if cut into the rampart; their roof was made of logs covered with the earth of the upper part of the rampart. Archaeologists have discovered a wide assortment of artefacts here: the arms and armour of professional warriors, farming implements, craftsmen's tools, and even women's jewellery. These artefacts show that the cells were used as living quarters and storerooms. Ramparts with such cells occurred in areas where over-ground dwellings were widespread, as well as where semi-dugouts were still built.

For a long time the opinions of researchers differed with regard to the social nature of settlements with cells in the ramparts. Because of their structural peculiarities they were considered first to be feudal castles, then fortresses where the cells were occupied by servants or warrior-farmers who engaged in farming in peace but kept horses and weapons at the ready. A recent investigation by A. V. Kuza shows that settlements with such cells varied greatly both in size (from 0.1 to more than 20 hectares) and layout (some conformed to the terrain, others had a complex layout, more characteristic of cities). In other words, the structural peculiarities were not distinctive of a certain type of *gorodishche*, or a certain period of time, or settlements with approximately the same number of inhabitants. The only feature they have in common is the presence of a vast unfortified *possad* beyond their fortifications. Therefore, it may be suggested that cells in ramparts served as a refuge for the population of the *possad* in time of danger. Similar small cells designed to be used in case of a siege and called *osadnaya klet'* and *osadny dvor* became common in fortresses in the 16th and 17th centuries.

The defence capacity of a fortress directly depended on its stores of water. Russian fortresses were not provided with big water tanks for gathering rainwater; in times of impending siege, water was stored in barrels, which were filled by hand; their size was a limiting factor. Sometimes a river branch or a channel ran through the so-called water-gate of a fortress. This method was not foolproof, though, as the besiegers could build a dam and divert the water away. The safest source of water supply was having a well inside the fortress. However, a low water table or hard ground could make this impossible. In these circumstances, a special feature called a *tainik* (from the word *taina* meaning 'secret') was resorted to. A *tainik* was a secret underground passage running down a hill slope towards the river, or a natural spring, or a place where a well could be easily dug. In order to build a *tainik*, an open trench was first dug out and then roofed over, covered with earth, and camouflaged with turf. *Tainik* exits were also carefully camouflaged and guarded. For instance, a stone-laid *tainik* in Izborsk was a 40m-long underground passage leading to a spring. The latter was encircled by a log shell and camouflaged. Nevertheless, it was discovered by the Livonians in 1341. The latter destroyed the *tainik* and deprived the defenders of water. The Livonians, however, did not know that it was the defenders' only source of water, and faced with furious resistance thought it better to retreat.

Until the late 15th century the entrance to a *tainik* was situated right next to the wall of the fortress. Later it led out from the tower nearest to the river. The tower was then called a *tainichnaya* (or *tainitskaya*) *bashnya*.

The entrance to the *tainik* in Izborsk fortress, viewed from the interior. This underground, stone-laid passage that led to a spring was about 40m long. The exit from the *tainik* and the spring were enclosed in a wooden log shell and camouflaged. In 1341, however, the Livonians discovered the *tainik* and cut off the defenders' water supply.

The sites at war

Territorial gain never was the objective of the nomadic warriors, the main enemy facing Rus' in the 10th to 12th centuries. Their lightning raids on horseback were aimed at capturing prisoners, cattle and property, before beating a rapid retreat back to the steppe. In their retaliatory punitive expeditions, the Russian princes tried to debilitate the enemy, seizing booty and preventing possible future attacks. Neither the nomads nor the Russians readily resorted to sieges. For instance, during the period between 1060 and 1237 only one in every five armed clashes was centred around capturing a fortified settlement.

Until the 12th century the most common method of capturing a fortified settlement was a surprise raid called an *iz'yezd* or *izgon*. An *iz'yezd* was carried out by piling through a gate that the defenders had been unable to bar in time. Numerous instances of this prove that patrolling was poorly executed by the defenders, and watch-towers were an exception rather than the rule.

When a fortified settlement could not be taken by surprise attack, it was either passed by or a passive siege (i.e. a blockade, or *oblezhanie*) was laid to it. The aim was to force the besieged to surrender for lack of food or water, and to this end the fortified settlement was surrounded and cut off from the outside world. *Oblezhanie* was practised both by the Pecheneg and Polovtsy nomads and the Russians. The best-known siege laid by the nomads to a Russian city is the *oblezhanie* of Kiev in 968. On the evidence of Russian chroniclers, a large Pecheneg army encircled the city so thoroughly that neither beast nor bird could get in or out of it. Provisions and water ran out, and the situation was only saved by Prince Svyatoslav, who came to the rescue at the head of his army. In the struggle to take the throne of Kiev, not once did Prince Vladimir take a fortress by storm; he always used blockades.

A direct assault on a fortress was known in Russian chronicles as a *vzyatie kop'yom*, and this became popular only in the second half of the 12th century. Primitive devices were used during such assaults, such as bundles of wood for filling up ditches, and scaling ladders for climbing walls. The first mention of throwing machines (*poroks*) is made in this period; they were not widespread until the 13th century though. The main weapons of the defenders, apart from arrows, were stones and logs thrown down from the walls on the assailants.

The main attack was usually made on the gate, and understandably so. Gates were cut into the rampart and it was easier to attack them than the walls standing on a high earthen rampart. It is interesting that in settlements of a complex layout, where the external site (*okol'ny gorod*) was never protected by

OPPOSITE The siege of Vladimir by the Mongols, February 6, 1238
On February 3 the Mongols led by Batu Khan approached the city. After surrounding it with a palisade, they set up their throwing machines. While preparing for the assault, Batu Khan sent a detached corps to capture Suzdal. Being insufficiently manned, it was seized straight away and by February 6 the corps had already returned to the walls of Vladimir. Meanwhile the besiegers kept up their bombardment of the urban fortifications around the Golden Gate. The upper parts of the walls (*zaborola*) were destroyed in some places, while in others the wooden walls were completely pulled down. By the evening of February 6 the Mongols had filled up the ditch and rushed into the breaches. The defenders resisted fiercely and the attack was beaten off. Early the next day, however, the assault was resumed and by noon the outer fortifications had succumbed. The inhabitants took refuge in 'Monomakh's city' and in the *detinets*, but these, too, were soon captured by the enemy. The prince's family, boyars, and common people who had sought refuge in the cathedral were all burned alive as the Mongols set fire to it. Thus, on February 7, 1238, the capital of the Vladimir-Suzdal principality fell to the Mongols.

The siege of Vladimir by the Mongols, February 6, 1238

a rampart on the side of the *detinets* (citadel) and the rampart of the external site never adjoined the ramparts of the *detinets*, the most vulnerable place (the ditch between the *okol'ny gorod* and the *detinets*) was never subjected to attack. One might assume, though, that by following the bottom of this ditch (which may have been barred with obstacles) it would be easy to take the *okol'ny gorod*. However, the attackers would probably suffer very heavy losses moving along the ditch and climbing its slope in the direction of the *okol'ny gorod*: they would find themselves under crossfire from both the *okol'ny gorod* and from the walls of the *detinets*.

The Mongol invasion of 1237–40 proved a serious test for the Russian fortresses. The Mongols would first surround a city with earth and timber siege works (palisades or ramparts, or both) and mount throwing machines. The latter were usually placed in batteries facing the most vulnerable sections where a breach (usually more than one) was to be made. The throwing machines would then begin a day-and-night continuous assault. Stone-throwers tried not only to breach a wall but also to destroy the upper *zaborola* on the adjoining sections, thus suppressing any fire from the defenders. The Mongols then would set about filling up the ditches. This was carried out by the civilian population brought by force from the neighbouring towns and villages. If one of them failed to deliver the necessary material into the ditch or to the wall, he was killed. When the ditch was filled, the assault began. Here, too, captured civilians were made use of. The storming columns quite often drove them ahead of the troops as a sort of first wave. This ruthless method served not only to protect the Mongolian warriors but also to unnerve the defenders. All these siege methods were demonstrated in the siege of Vladimir by the Mongols in 1238.

The defenders of Russian fortified cities had little with which to withstand the onslaught of the Mongol armies. Wooden fortifications were easily destroyed both by stone-throwing engines and fire. With the *zaborolas* knocked off the walls, the besieged could not even effectively defend themselves with arrows. A lack of stone-throwing engines meant they were unable to destroy the siege weapons of the Mongols. Sorties were difficult because of the siege line and numerical superiority of the Mongols. As a result many Russian cities and towns, even well fortified ones, took but a few (usually four to six) days to fall.

However, some fortresses offered up staunch resistance and some were not taken at all. The defence of Kozelsk in 1238 is a famous example. The little town put up heroic resistance to the huge army of Batu Khan for seven long weeks. In the interim the Mongols kept the town under constant fire from throwing machines. The inhabitants, for their part, made sorties to destroy the enemy siege weapons. The Mongols finally managed to destroy the walls and made a direct assault. The inhabitants fought back using whatever weapons and tools were to hand, including kitchen knives. Moments later a group of the besieged made a sortie and killed about 4,000 enemy soldiers in a surprise attack. The Mongols did eventually take the town but only after all the soldiers and men defending it had been killed; after that they slaughtered all of the remaining civilian population. The events were such a shock to the Mongols that they never after referred to the town by its proper name, but nicknamed it 'Wicked Town'.

Some fortresses proved too strong for the Mongols, particularly those built on hills. Shooting at an upward angle rendered stone-throwers almost useless. The Mongols were not able to destroy the walls of the Kolodyazhin fortress, which sat on a hill, and only took it by resorting

The ramparts and ditches of Izheslavl (Izyaslavl of Ryazan) were destroyed and burned down by the Mongolian hordes of Batu Khan. On its most vulnerable sides the settlement was protected with three rows of ramparts and ditches. The ramparts were topped with wooden walls.

to a ruse. Realizing that it was hopeless to take the Volhynia fortresses Kremenets and Danilov, they made no attempt to besiege them and passed them by.

While north-east and south Rus' became acquainted with the siege methods of Mongols, north-west Rus' came up against western European siege techniques. Here the Germans often besieged Russian fortresses, using approximately the same assortment of siege weapons as the Mongols.

In the early 13th century the regular laying of sieges, and thus the use of complex siege weapons, was still a new skill for the Russians. However, by the mid 13th century they became expert in both and laid quick and successful sieges.

The rampart and the white-stone Golden Gate of Vladimir. These defences protected the western *possad* of the city, the so-called Novy Gorod (New City). It was roughly in this sector that the main thrust of the Mongolian assault was directed in February 1238. At that date, the rampart was topped with log cell walls and the Golden Gate looked rather different.

It is interesting to highlight a few statistics on this matter. In the sources 302 military conflicts are registered between 1228 and 1462: 171 relate to sieges or the defence of fortified settlements, and only 85 relate to field battles. Such a sharp increase in the number of sieges compared to field battles is not accidental and is connected with new strategic aims. Both the Mongols and Germans aimed to capture territory and keep it for years to come. Later on, the same goals were pursued by the Russians in their quest to unite their different principalities. Complete control over territory was only possible once all the centres of resistance had been suppressed. This brought sieges to the fore.

It is also interesting to compare the number of successful and unsuccessful sieges laid by Russian and foreign armies (Mongols, Germans, and others). Data on two Russian regions (north and south) are given in Table 1. The most interesting fact is that the number of successful and unsuccessful sieges remains roughly the same irrespective of who actually laid the siege – despite the advanced siege techniques of the Mongols and the large number of cities taken by them. Only one out of every five besieged cities successfully resisted the siege. The coefficient is at its maximum (4.38) for the sieges laid by the Russians – proving that the Russians had been quick to master siege methods and had become expert in siege warfare.

Table 1: The instances of siege and defence of fortresses between 1228 and 1462.

	North Rus'	South Rus'	Total	Correlation of successful and unsuccessful sieges
Sieges laid by the Russians				
Successful sieges	50	7	57	4.38
Unsuccessful sieges	12	1	13	
Defence of cities and fortresses by the Russians				
Unsuccessful defence	70	11	81	4.05
Successful defence	17	3	20	
Total number of captured cities	120	18	138	4.18
Total number of unsuccessful sieges	29	4	33	

49

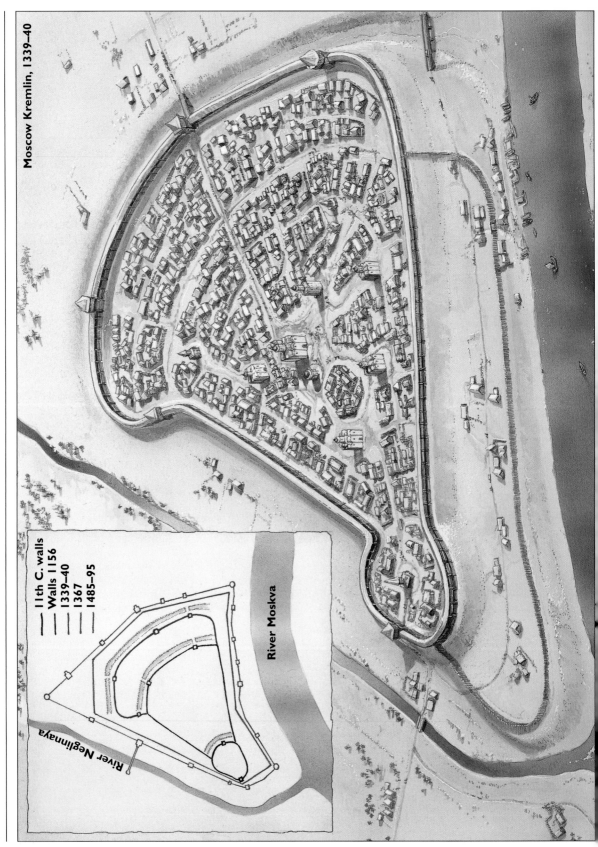

Moscow Kremlin, 1339–40

11th C. walls
Walls 1156
1339–40
1367
1485–95

River Neglinnaya

River Moskva

OPPOSITE **Moscow Kremlin, 1339–40**

The main part of this illustration shows a reconstruction of the Moscow Kremlin as it looked in 1339–40; the top left plan details the evolution of Moscow's fortifications from the 11th to the 15th century. Moscow grew up around Prince Yuri Dolgoruki's castle, although a settlement on the promontory at the confluence of the rivers Moskva and Neglinnaya had existed previously. The 11th-century fortifications consisted of an earthen rampart topped with a palisade. A ditch, probably a dry one, was dug out on the mainland side. In 1156 the castle was fortified anew in compliance with the order of Prince Yuri Dolgoruki. The new fortifications comprised a rampart with wooden walls on top. Two gates led into the castle: one on the mainland side and the other at the tip of the promontory. The site protected by these defences was five or six times larger than the original one. In the late 12th through the 13th centuries Moscow's fortifications were destroyed and then restored at least twice. The fortress was first burned down by the army of Prince Gleb of Ryazan in 1177 and then by the Mongols in 1237/38. The great fires of 1331 and 1337 destroyed all the fortifications, and new ones were raised in 1339–40. The 2–6m-thick walls, made of oak logs about 70cm in diameter, now embraced a larger site, stretching for 1.67km. An important innovation was the towers, which stood up to 13m high, whereas earlier fortifications could only boast gate-towers. The towers were generally concentrated on the mainland side. The oak-wood *kremlin* lasted no more than 26 years; it was completely burned down in the fire of 1365. The next year the decision was taken to build a new, this time stone, *kremlin*, erected in 1367. Its walls of white stone were 2–3m thick, nearly 2km long, and were strengthened by eight or nine towers distributed along the perimeter. The latter *kremlin* lasted until the late 15th century when between 1485 and 1495 it was modernized and acquired the brick walls that can be seen today, with little change since then.

Which siege weapons and methods were used by the Russians? Fire and axes had been the main weapons of attack from ancient times, and many miniatures show Russian soldiers setting fire to the walls of a besieged fortress or chopping down fortifications with their axes. Fire arrows were almost certainly used too. Siege towers (*tury*) were not popular and battering rams are very rarely mentioned.

Throwing machines (*poroks*) are mentioned in the chronicles 130 times. The first evidence in the sources dates from 1184 when the Polovtsy attempted to use a great crossbow. In the early 13th century, even before the Mongol invasion, the Russians certainly knew of throwing machines and used them occasionally, but they did not become popular until the mid 13th century. Their appearance brought certain changes in fortifications, such as the gradual replacement of wooden walls by stone ones and the use of multiple rows of ramparts and ditches.

Izborsk fortress, founded in 1303. By 1330 its wooden walls had already been replaced with stone ones. The only tower the fortress had at that time, the Lukovka, became a donjon inside the fortress walls.

Man-powered and counterweight engines were without doubt the main type of stone-throwers, and were used by the Mongols, the Germans, and the Russians. However, some illustrations in the Russian annals represent stone-throwers of an altogether different type – great crossbows that fired stones instead of bolts. These miniatures depict events that took place in the 13th century, but themselves were made in the 16th century when throwing machines had gone out of use. These machines may have been but the fruit of the artist's imagination, but they may also have been copied from an earlier source that has not been preserved to our day. On the basis of a detailed analysis of the miniatures it has been suggested that two structures probably existed and reconstructions of them have been attempted.[1] One engine had a solid frame with a groove and the other had a slide.

Cannon appeared in Rus' in the 1370–80s. The first mention of firearms in Russian chronicles dates from 1382 when the defenders of Moscow used *tyufyaks* (a small cannon of the howitzer type, which fired case-shot), along with throwing-machines, against Tokhtamysh Khan. Initially the use of cannon was confined to sieges and the defence of fortresses. Until the mid 15th century cannon and throwing-machines co-existed. It

The siege of Kozelsk by the Mongols in 1238. This miniature was made in the 16th century, much later than the date of the event. Thus, the fortress and the armament of the warriors date from the 16th not the 13th century. This miniature is, however, one of but a few showing great crossbows used in besieging a fortress. Curiously enough, here they shoot stones not bolts. These stationary crossbows may have been purely imaginary, but they may also have been copied from an earlier source. (Golitsin's volume of Nikon's annals)

was only in the mid 15th century that the destructive power of cannon surpassed that of throwing machines and the decline of the latter began. 1446 saw the first city fall to cannon fire, although its wall was not destroyed. The first instance of a stone wall destroyed by cannon fire dates from 1481.

Sometimes a city was taken by stealth. The best known stratagem was resorted to by Princess Olga in 946 at the siege of the Drevlyan's city of Iskorosten. The siege was a long one, but the city would not surrender. Then Princess Olga started peace negotiations promising to lift the siege on condition that the inhabitants deliver to her three doves and three sparrows from each *dvor*. The defenders were surprised, but wishing the siege to be lifted, agreed. When the birds were brought to Princess Olga, she ordered that a piece of tinder be tied to each bird. When it grew dark the pieces of tinder were set on fire and the birds were let out. They flew to their own nests in the city and soon it was all in flames. The story may be nothing but a legend. However, there is no smoke without fire. Even Kautilya, the author of the ancient Indian treatise *Arthashastra*, recommended tying burning material to birds' tails and letting them fly to the enemy fortresses (Art. XIII, 4, 174–75).

[1] Kirpichnikov, A. N., 'Metatelnaya artilleriya drevnei Rusi', *Materialy i issledovaniya po arkheologii SSSR*, 77, p.7–51 (Moscow, 1958).

Aftermath

A large number of fortified settlements ceased to exist as early as the 10th and 11th centuries. Some of the *gorods* disappeared as a result of the expansion and strengthening of Kievan Rus'. Kievan princes took tough measures against seats of tribal separatism. Nomad raids proved fatal to many settlements in the 11th century, while others were burned down in internal strife. Even if the inhabitants were lucky enough to survive and returned to the ruins, they often abandoned the old fortified settlement for whatever reason and built a new one some distance away. Not all the fortified settlements, however, were destroyed in war. Some of those in the interior of Kievan Rus' were considered superfluous and abandoned. The inhabitants moved to unfortified settlements better suited to everyday living, believing that the state armed forces, the Zmievy Valy and the frontier fortresses would offer sufficient protection against nomadic warriors. A small group of fortified settlements vanished altogether around the turn of the 11th/12th century. This was a transition period from early feudalism to its mature stage; rapidly developing cities or castles attracted people in nearby settlements to the centres of political and economic life, and the deserted settlements fell into decay.

The devastating Mongol invasion of 1237–40 proved fatal for a great number of settlements. Two out of every three Russian cities were burned down, and a third of those destroyed were abandoned forever. Even more devastating were the consequences for smaller settlements, such as castles, fortresses, and villages. Three out of four of these were fully destroyed and only one out of four such settlements lived to see the 14th century.

Given that many of the fortifications in the period under discussion were timber and earth, little of them survives today. Most of the *gorodishches* that survive are merely vacant plots of land, surrounded by ramparts and ditches covered in grass – the telltale clue as to their former status. Some ramparts have been so eroded that once formidable fortifications are hard to recognize. Others, however, survive to a fair height. Considerable lengths of impressive

Remains of the Nikolskaya Tower, Izborsk fortress. It was raised in the 17th century at the end of the Nikolski *zakhab*, a long passage between the fortress walls that improved the defences of the entrance. The walls of the *zakhab* survive only in small sections.

The Golden Gate in Vladimir built supposedly in the mid 12th century. It was flanked with buttresses enclosed in small circular towers and had its upper part together with the church completely rebuilt in the late 18th/early 19th centuries.

ramparts have been preserved in certain cities (for example, in Vladimir, Pereyaslavl-Ryazanski, and other places), although the adjoining ground on either side of them was long ago built over with modern houses.

The stone gates granted to some cities still survive, usually guarding the city's symbol. The presence of chapels has aided their preservation. The Golden Gate in Vladimir was the pride not only of the city but of the entire Vladimir principality. It was supposedly built in the mid 12th century as an imitation of the gate of Kiev. In Vladimir it was a rectangular gate-tower about 25m high with a chapel on top. The arch over the gateway was 14m high and featured shutters bound with leaves of gilt copper. The gate survives today, though little of its 12th-century appearance remains. In 1795 the weakened corners of the gate were strengthened with buttresses confined in circular towers. In 1810 the upper part of the gate was re-laid and a new chapel was built above the gate. Nothing is left of the battlemented parapet once girdling the tower. The Golden Gate in Kiev, however, fared worse, and nothing of it now survives: the gate was built anew in 1982.

The Zmievy Valy were abandoned for almost a thousand years, their initial function nearly forgotten. In the late 1920s, however, the Soviet military authorities decided to make fresh use of them for the protection of the southern borders of the Soviet Union. Some ramparts were turned into a fortified defensive line. Numerous permanent firing positions and concrete fortifications were built inside the ramparts. These defensive lines blocked the way of the German invaders in July 1941, and were fought over fiercely for 70 long days and nights. According to a German eyewitness, the Russian defence was 'worthy of the greatest praise, and the structures seem impossible to destroy'. Many centuries after their construction, the Zmievy Valy had served in the defence of their country once again.

The sites today

Some 1,500 fortified Russian settlements can be traced to the territories of modern Russia, Belarus, Ukraine, and Poland. Some fortifications have been fairly well preserved or reconstructed, others are only represented by grassy ramparts. Only the defences of the most important cites, the best-preserved fortresses, and the most interesting fortified settlements are (briefly) described below. The names of countries and sometimes districts are given in brackets to make it easier for the reader to locate the *gorodishches* on a map.

Belgorod (Belgorodka village, Kievan district, Ukraine)

The fortress was built in 991 to protect Kiev from nomadic raids. The *gorodishche*, comprising a *detinets* (citadel) and *okol'ny gorod,* is encircled by ramparts up to 5m high and up to 12m thick at the base. The ramparts are strengthened with an intra-rampart framework of oak log shells, mud-brick, and clay.

Borisov-Glebov (Romanovo-Borisoglebskoe *gorodishche*, Vakino village, Ryazan district, Russia)

First mentioned in the annals of 1180, it grew up on the site of an Iron Age settlement. Semi-circular in shape, the *gorodishche* is surrounded with three lines of ramparts and ditches and a side bordering the river.

Czartoryisk (Ukraine)

Ruins of a circular donjon-tower built in 1291.

Dmitrov (Moscow district, Russia)

The city was founded by Prince Yuri Dolgoruki in 1154. Its formidable ramparts survive.

Galich (Krylos village, Ivano-Frankovsk district, Ukraine)

The village houses a colossal *gorodishche* – the remains of Galich, capital of the Galich and later the Galich-Volhynia principality. Defences first appeared here as far back as the 10th century but the major fortifications were raised in the second half of the 12th century. The *detinets* (citadel) was protected on the mainland side by two rows of ramparts and ditches. Log walls crowned the high ramparts. The *okol'ny gorod* was encircled by as many as four lines of ditches and ramparts, the latter surmounted with wooden fortifications.

Gdov (Pskov district, Russia)

A stone fortress was founded here in 1431. The walls, made of alternating layers of boulders and limestone, were 4.3m thick, about 8m high, and 850m long. The fortress was provided with three gates with *zakhabs*, and with three towers. The gates and the towers do not survive and the height of the walls does not surpass 5.5m today.

BELOW LEFT The ruins of the walls of Gdov fortress. Their height is no more than 5.5m now. Built of alternating horizontal rows of boulders and limestone, this type of fortification is fairly rare.

BELOW RIGHT The ramparts of the *gorodishche* of Kideksha, a small castle built in the 12th century on the site of an earlier settlement. The white-stone church of St Boris and St Gleb was also built in the 12th century and is one of the oldest buildings of this kind in north-eastern Rus'.

Izheslavl (a village in Ryazan district, Russia)

Only ramparts and ditches are left of the fortified settlement laid waste by Mongols in 1237. It was once protected on three sides by three rows of ramparts and ditches. A *detinets* only 20 × 30m in size stood in a corner of the settlement protected by ramparts.

Kamenets (Belarus)

A five-storey (ground floor included) brick donjon built between 1271 and 1288 is well preserved here. It is the best surviving example of the characteristic towers of Volhynia.

Kideksha (a village 4km from Suzdal, Russia)

There are earthen ramparts and the white-stone church of St Boris and St Gleb still to be seen in the *gorodishche* (supposedly the residence of Prince Yuri Dolgoruki). The fortifications and the church were built in the 12th century.

Kiev (Ukraine)

A settlement existed here as far back as the Iron Age. In the 6th and 7th centuries there were several fortified Slavic settlements on the territory of the modern city. In 989 Prince Vladimir had the old defences levelled to the ground and new, much more formidable fortifications were raised to encircle an enlarged area. The new fortified centre, called 'Vladimir's city', was surrounded with ramparts 16m high and 9–13m thick at the base. The ramparts had an intra-rampart wooden framework and were topped with whitewashed wooden log walls. Four gates, some of them of stone and brick, led into the city. Even more formidable fortifications were raised in Kiev in the early 11th century by Prince Yaroslav. The protected territory ('Yaroslav's city') was seven times larger than 'Vladimir's city' and adjoined the latter on the south. The fortifications comprised powerful earthen ramparts (up to 16m high and 25–30m thick at the base) with wooden intra-rampart framework. They were topped with wooden log walls and stretched for 3.5km. Four stone or brick gates led into 'Yaroslav's city', the most famous being the Great (Golden) Gate. Before the invasion of the hordes of Batu Khan no other fortifications in Rus' could rival those of 'Yaroslav's city'. Remains of the gigantic ramparts of ancient Kiev can be seen today in the centre of the modern city. The Golden Gate with the adjoining sections of wooden walls was reconstructed in 1982.

Kleshchin (Gorodishche village, near Pereyaslavl-Zalesski, Russia)

A small (55 × 80m) fortress sat on a hill called Alexander's Mount with an unfortified settlement nearby. The fortress was encircled by a rampart topped with wooden walls. The ramparts are 3–8m high today.

Ladoga (Staraya Ladoga village, Russia)

Only fragments of walls of the stone fortress of 1114 survive, as in the 1490s the fortress was considerably modernized.

The rampart and ditch of Mstislavl. This settlement, roughly circular in plan, was probably a prince's castle. Today trees grow on top of the rampart, which was once topped with wooden walls.

Lutsk (Ukraine)

The brick walls and the towers of the citadel of the so-called Verkhni Zamok (Upper Castle) are well preserved. They were built in 1289–1321 on the place where the older wooden walls were destroyed in 1259 in compliance with the Mongols' order. The fortifications underwent modernization from 1430 to 1542. The fortifications of the *okol'ny gorod*, the so-called Nizhni Zamok (Lower Castle) – a rampart, a ditch, and a stone wall of the second half of the 14th century – survive in fragments.

Moscow (Russia)

Hardly anything is left of the fortifications of the Moscow Kremlin of the 12th–14th centuries. The *kremlin* we can see today was built in 1485–95 and rebuilt later (see Fortress 39: *Russian Fortresses*

1480–1682). Out of several *gorodishches* of the period in question discovered on the territory of the modern city, Dyakovskoye *gorodishche* on the site of Kolomenskoye Park is the one that is best known and most explored. It gave the name to an entire culture of the Iron Age – the Dyakovskaya Culture (the 8th–7th centuries BC to the 6th–7th centuries AD). A settlement existed on this site in the late 1st millennium BC through the 6th–7th centuries AD. The original defences (a rampart and a ditch) were modernized at the turn of the 11th/12th century when the *gorodishche* became a feudal castle.

Mstislavl (Gorodishche village, about 10km from the town of Yuriev-Polski, Russia)

A rampart and a moat survive of the fortifications of a settlement founded in the second half of the 12th–early 13th centuries. The rampart strengthened with an oak intra-rampart structure reaches 6m in height and 32m in thickness at the base. The settlement was nearly circular in plan and was probably a prince's castle.

Pereyaslavl (now Pereyaslav-Khmelnitski, Ukraine)

Within the confines of the modern town of Pereyaslav-Khmelnitski there is a colossal *gorodishche* – the remains of the once great city of Pereyaslavl. Pereyaslavl's fortifications comprised a *detinets* and an *okol'ny gorod*; both were enclosed in a high rampart, strengthened with an intra-rampart wooden structure, and topped with a wooden wall. A wide and deep ditch ran in front of the rampart.

Pereyaslavl (Pereyaslavl-Zalesski, now Pereslavl-Zalesski, Russia)

The city was founded by Prince Yuri Dolgoruki in 1152. Its fortifications consisted of formidable ramparts. Based on wooden cells and topped with wooden log walls, they were 2.35km long. The ramparts are well preserved and even today are imposing: they are 10m high and 30m thick at the base.

Poyarkovo (a village in Ryazan district, Russia)

Opposite the village, on the other bank of the River Zhraka, lies a *gorodishche* of the 12th–13th centuries. It was protected by three rows of ramparts and ditches. The innermost rampart goes along the entire perimeter of the settlement, while the two outer ones run down the riverbank and stop at the river. Today the ramparts are 7m high and the ditches are 2m deep.

Ryazan (Pereyaslavl-Ryazanski, Russia)

Earlier known as Pereyaslavl-Ryazanski, the city became the capital of the Ryazan principality in the mid 14th century. In 1778 it was renamed Ryazan. The city's *kremlin* was enclosed by a strong rampart topped with oak walls. The fortifications were modernized up to the mid 17th century. Only a 220m-long and 12m-high section of the earthen rampart survives. *Gorodishche* Staraya Ryazan (Old Ryazan), the remains of the old capital of the Ryazan principality, is to be found 65km south-east of modern Ryazan.

Stolpie (Poland)

Ruins of a rectangular stone donjon of the 13th century can be seen here.

Suzdal (Russia)

The city was first mentioned in the annals of 1024. One can see the ramparts of the *detinets* today: they are 1.4km long, 3.2–8.5m high and 35m thick at the base. When built under Vladimir Monomakh at the turn of the 11th/12th century, they were up to 10m high and topped with wooden walls. In the late 12th and the second half of the 15th centuries the ramparts were strengthened and built up with earth. The year 1677 saw a new pinewood wall with 15 towers and gates built on top of them. However, all the wooden fortifications burned down in the fire of 1719.

A 220m-long section of the rampart is all that remains of the fortifications of Pereyaslavl-Ryazanski, capital of the Ryazan principality from the mid 14th century. With wooden walls surmounting the rampart even the domes of the churches were not visible from beyond the fortifications.

Tustan (1km to the north-east of the village of Urych, Lvov district, Ukraine)

The most famous of the rock fortresses of Galicia. In the 13th and 14th centuries an earlier settlement known from the 10th–11th centuries was turned into a powerful fortress. Its citadel (called *Kamen* or 'Stone') sat on a small ground between four rocks towering 51m above the valley. The citadel comprised five-storey (ground floor included) living quarters and wooden log defensive walls with towers about 15m high. The storeys were connected by a complex system of passages and stairs. A stone wall was raised on the southern side. A *possad* protected with ramparts, ditches, and wooden walls lay at the foot of the citadel on the slopes of the mountain. A stone-paved road leading to the gate of the citadel ran along the bottom of the ditch. One kilometre from the city, on the rocks of the Ostry Kamen (Sharp Rock) and the Malaya Skala (Small Rock), there was a watch post suited to carrying on independent defensive activities: wooden walls protected the approaches to the rocks and a tank 2m in diameter and 8m deep was placed on the top of the Ostry Kamen.

Vladimir (Russia)

The city was founded by Vladimir Monomakh in 1108. Large-scale construction work was under way here in 1158–65. By the end of the 12th century Vladimir had four sites protected by walls: a *detinets*, Monomakh's city (the Middle City), and two fortified *possads* on the latter's sides. The *detinets* was encircled in rather thin (1.0–1.7m) stone walls. All the defences with the exception of the walls of the *detinets* and several gates were of timber and earth; they consisted of a ditch and a rampart surmounted with a wooden wall. The ramparts were about 8m high and 24m thick at the base. Some sections of ramparts and the famous stone Golden Gate survive now, although the latter has undergone considerable modernization.

Yuriev-Polski (Russia)

A 1km-long rampart surrounded a town nearly round in plan. Preserved from the 12th century, the rampart is 7m high and 12m thick at the base.

The ramparts and ditches are all that remains of the fortifications of Suzdal built by Vladimir Monomakh at the turn of the 11th/12th century.

OPPOSITE **Kiev in the 12th–13th centuries**

The main part of this illustration shows a general outlay of Kiev's fortifications (after P. P. Tolochko). In 989 Prince Vladimir fortified the central part of the city thus creating the so-called 'Vladimir's city' (**1**). The fortifications consisted of formidable earthen ramparts topped with whitewashed wooden log walls. Among the four gate-towers the St Sophia Gate (**2**, after Yu. S. Aseev) was notable, being the first gate in Rus' built of brick and stone, not of wood. Under Prince Yaroslav the southern part of the city saw itself encircled by strong fortifications and acquired the name of 'Yaroslav's city' (**3**). Until Batu Khan's invasion these fortifications were the most powerful in Rus'. They comprised 3.5km of huge earthen ramparts provided with wooden intra-rampart structures and topped with wooden walls. Out of the four gates the Golden Gate (**4**, after S. A. Vysotski), which served as a model for similar gates in other Russian cities (for example, in Pereyaslavl and Vladimir), is worth a special mention. The height of the gateway arch exceeded 12m and its width was almost 7m. The gate shutters were made of oak, forged with iron and bound with leaves of gilt copper. The gate was topped with a church, which had a golden dome. The building of the fortifications of 'Yaroslav's city' took 15–20 years, and was completed in 1037.

Bibliography and further reading

No comprehensive works on early Russian fortresses have so far been published in English. Therefore, almost all the books listed below are written in Russian.

Antonovich, V. B., 'Zmievy valy v predelah Kievskoi zemli (Snake Ramparts inside the Boundaries of the Kiev District)', *Kievskaya starina (Kievan Old Times)*, March (1884).

Arkheologiya SSSR, Drevnyaya Rus'. Gorod, zamok, selo (Archaeology of the USSR, Old Rus'. Town, Castle, Village) (Moscow, 1985).

Bugai, A. S., 'Zmievy valy Kievshchiny (Zmievy Valy in the Kiev district), *Ukr. Ist. zhurnal* (Ukrainian Historical Journal), 6, p.74–83 (Kiev, 1970).

Gimbutas, M., *The Slavs* (London, 1971).

Gulyanitskii, N. F. (ed.), *Drevnerusskoye gradostroitel'stvo X – XV veka* (Ancient Russian Town-planning, 10th–15th centuries) (Moscow, 1993).

Ivanov, Yu. G., *Starinnye kreposti Rossii* (Old Fortresses of Russia) (Smolensk, 2004).

Ivanov, Yu. G., *Velikiye kreposti Rossii* (The Great Fortresses of Russia) (Smolensk, 2004).

Khrapachevski, R. P., *Voennaya derzhava Chingizhana* (The Military Power of Genghis Khan) (Moscow, 2004).

Kirpichnikov, A. N., *Kamennyye kreposti Novgorodskoy zemli* (The Stone Fortresses of the Novgorod District) (Leningrad, 1984).

Kirpichnikov, A. N., 'Metatelnaya artilleriya drevnei Rusi' (Throwing-artillery in Old Rus'), *Materialy i issledovaniya po arkheologii SSSR* (Materials and Investigations on Archaeology in the USSR), 77, p.7–51 (Moscow, 1958).

Kostochkin, V. V., *Drevnerusskiye goroda. Pamyatniki zodchestva XI – XVII vekov* (Ancient Russian Towns. The Monuments of Architecture, 11th–17th centuries) (Moscow, 1972).

Kostochkin, V. V., *Drevniye russkiye kreposti* (Ancient Russian Fortresses) (Moscow, 1964).

Kostochkin, V. V., *Krepostnoye zodchestvo drevney Rusi* (The Military Architecture of Ancient Rus') (Moscow, 1969).

Kostochkin, V. V., *Russkoye oboronnoye zodchestvo kontsa XIII – nachala XVI vekov* (Russian Defence Architecture, the End of 13th–Beginning of 16th Century) (Moscow, 1962).

Kowalczyk, E., 'Waly Zmijowe'(Zmievy Valy), *'Kwartalnik Historii Kultury Materialnej*, (Quarterly Journal of the History of Cultural Artefacts) 17, 2 (1969).

Kradin, N. P., *Russkoye derevyannoye oboronnoye zodchestvo* (Russian Wooden Defence Architecture) (Moscow, 1988).

Kuchera, M. P., *Zmievy valy Srednego Podneprov'ya* (Snake Ramparts of the District in the Mid-stream of the Dnieper) (Kiev, 1987).

Kuza, A. V., *Drevnerusskiye gorodishcha X–XIII.* (Old Russian Gorodishches of the 10th–13th Centuries) (Moscow, 1996).

Kyui, Ts., *Kratki istoricheski ocherk dolgovremennoi fortifikatsii v Rossii* (A Short Historical Essay on Long-standing Fortifications in Russia) (St Petersburg, 1897).

Laskovskii, F., *Materialy dlya Istorii Ingenernogo Iskusstva v Rossii* (Materials for the History of the Engineering Art in Russia), 3 vols (St Petersburg, 1858–65).

Nicolle, D., *Medieval Warfare. Source Book. Christian Europe and its Neighbours* (London, 1998).

Nicolle, D., *Armies of Medieval Russia, 750–1250* (Osprey Publishing, Oxford, 1999).

Nicolle, D., Shpakovsky V., *Medieval Russian Armies, 1250–1500* (Osprey Publishing, Oxford, 2002)

Nossov, K. S., *Russkiye kreposti i osadnaya tekhnika VIII–XVII vekov* (Russian Fortresses and Siege Warfare, 8th–17th centuries) (St Petersburg and Moscow, 2003).

Rabinovich, M. G., 'Osadnaya tekhnika na Rusi v X–XV vekah' (Siege Weapons in Rus' in the 10th–15th Centuries), *Izvestiya AN SSSR. Seria istorii i filosofii* (News from the Academy of Sciences of the USSR. Series of History and Philosophy), 8, 1. p.61–75 (1951).

Rappoport, P. A., *Drevniye russkiye kreposti* (Ancient Russian Fortresses) (Moscow, 1965).

Rappoport, P. A., 'Ocherki po istorii voyennogo zodchestva Severo-Vostochnoy i Severo-Zapadnoy Rusi X – XV vekov (Essays on the History of Military Architecture of North-East and North-West Rus', 10–15th centuries)', *Materialy i issledovaniya po arkheologii SSSR* (Materials and Investigations on Archaeology in the USSR), 105, p.1–244 (Moscow and Leningrad, 1961).

Samoilovs'ki, I. M., 'Pereyaslavs'ki Zmiyovy vali' (Zmievy Valy of Pereyaslavl district), *Ukr. Ist. zhurnal* (Ukrainian Historical Journal), 3, p.101–02 (Kiev, 1971).

Soloviyov, S. M., *Istoriya Rossii s drevneishih vremyon* (History of Russia from Ancient Times), 4 vols (Moscow, 1988).

Voronin, N. N., 'Krepostnye sooruzheniya' (Fortress defensive works), *Istoriya kul'tury drevnei Rusi* (History of the Culture of Old Rus'), Vol.1 (Moscow and Leningrad, 1951).

Voronin, N. N., 'Moscovski Kreml' (1156–1367)' (The Moscow Kremlin), *Materials and Investigations on Archaeology in the USSR*), 77, p.52–66 (1958).

The Vyshka and Ryabinovka towers are situated on the most vulnerable, mainland side of the fortress of Izborsk. They projected far beyond the line of the walls, providing effective flanking fire. The loopholes, arranged in a fan-like manner, eliminated dead ground for the defenders.

Glossary

bashnya　A tower. The term appeared in the 16th century, replacing the earlier words *kostyor*, *strel'nitsa* and *vezha*.

boevoy hod　A wall-walk.

chastokol　A palisade, or wall of wooden stakes arranged vertically or obliquely in a row.

detinets　A citadel. The term was widely used up to the 14th century; later it was used only in the Novgorod principalities. It was replaced by the term *kremlin* in the Moscow and Tver principalities, and by the term *krom* in the Pskov principality.

dvor　A rural castle, or a town estate, or a courtyard.

gorod (or grad)　A fortified settlement, or defensive walls, or a fortification as a whole.

gorodishche　Surviving remains of a fortified settlement.

gorodni　Log cells of a wooden wall, placed side by side.

izgon　See *iz'yezd*.

iz'yezd　The capture of a fortified settlement by surprise attack.

kostyor　The word for a tower, common in the Pskov and Novgorod principalities until the 16th century.

kremlin　A fortress in a city (citadel). The term appeared in the 14th century (first mentioned in the annals of 1331) and replaced the earlier term *detinets* in the Moscow and Tver principalities.

krepost'　A fortress. The term appeared in the 17th century in place of the earlier term *gorod*.

krom　A citadel. The term appeared in the 14th century and was used in the Pskov principality in place of the earlier term *detinets*.

krovat'　A wooden planked wall-walk by a palisade wall.

nadvratnaya bashnya　A gate-tower.

oblam (oblom)　An overhanging projection in the upper part of a wooden wall or a tower, a kind of machicolation. Sometimes used as a synonym of *zaborola*.

oblezhanie　A passive siege, or blockade.

okhaben　A city suburb not fortified with walls.

okol'ny gorod　A fortified suburb outside a citadel's walls. This term can also refer to the external line of urban fortifications.

osadnaya klet'　A very small room used in the same way as an *osadny dvor*.

osadny dvor　A small room in a *kremlin* used for living in or for keeping the most valuable property of the nobility and monasteries during a siege.

osyp'　An earthen rampart.

pechura　A box-room with an embrasure, for placing a cannon in a tower or a wall.

persi　Literally, 'the breast'; in fortifications, a semi-circular (D-shaped) tower. In the Pskov citadel the name 'Persi' was given to the rampart on the most vulnerable, mainland side.

polati　A wall-walk on a palisade wall (also known as a *krovat'*).

porok　A throwing machine (siege weapon).

possad　A settlement populated by craftsmen and traders outside the walls of a citadel.

prikladka　External masonry built for the purpose of fortifying a wall.

pryaslo　The part of a fortress wall between two towers (a curtain wall).

selo　An unfortified rural settlement.

stolp　A tower not usually connected with a fortress's walls but free-standing. The term was used until the 16th century.

strel'nitsa　The word for a tower, common in the Moscow district until the 16th century.

tainichnaya (also tainitskaya) bashnya　A tower where the entrance to a *tainik* was situated.

ainik   An underground corridor leading out of a fortress and down the slope of a hill to a river, or a natural spring, or to a level where it was easy to dig a well.

arassy   The structure of log walls with longitudinal logs overlapping each other with the help of single cross-wise walls. Unlike the *gorodni* the *tarassy* structure was a solid wall, not separate log cells joined together. *Tarassy* were first mentioned in the annals of 1553.

ury   Siege towers.

yn   See *chastokol*.

yufyak   A small cannon of the howitzer type, which fired case-shot.

lapu   The way of joining logs at the corners so that their ends did not stick out beyond the external surface of the wall.

oblo   The way of joining logs at the corners so that their ends stuck out beyond the external surface of the wall.

ezha   A tower.

es' (pl. vesi)   An unfortified rural settlement, or village.

oivode   The commander of a Russian army or governor of a province.

ylaz   A secret exit from a fortress used to make sorties during a siege.

zyatie kop'yom   A direct assault on a fortress, as opposed to a siege.

aborola (zabrala)   The projecting upper part of a wall covered with a roof and overhanging the lower part of the wall (like a hoarding). The term is sometimes considered to be a synonym of *oblam*, or even to denote a wall in general.

akhab   A type of barbican.

amok   A castle. The word appeared in the Russian language comparatively late and is a derivative from the Polish *zamek*.

Even today the rampart of Pereyaslavl (Pereyaslavl-Zalesski) is 10m high and 30m thick at its base. With wooden walls on top, it represented a formidable defensive structure.

Index

References to illustrations are shown in **bold**.